# THE DAVIDIC PRINCE IN
# THE LAST DAYS

BY

DAUID YASHAR'EL YAHUDAH

# TABLE OF CONTENTS

# DEDICATION

*To the scattered remnant of yashar'el,*
*Whose awakening marks the fulfillment of prophecy.*

This book is dedicated to the sons and daughters of Yashar'el—those scattered across the earth, those carried into captivity, those lost among the nations, those whose names and lineages were forgotten by men but never forgotten by Yahuah. It is dedicated to every descendant of the ancient tribes whose ancestors endured slavery, colonization, dispersion, exile, and erasure, yet whose spirit could never be extinguished.

To those whose history was rewritten, whose culture was stripped away, whose identity was buried beneath centuries of silence— yet whose awakening in this generation fulfills the words of the prophets.

It is for the ones who heard the call of Yahuah in their hearts— to return, to repent, to remember, to walk again in covenant, to embrace the laws, commandments, and testimonies given to our fathers Abraham, Isaac, and Jacob.
It is dedicated to:
- The humble and faithful
- The seekers of truth
- The keepers of Torah
- The mothers and fathers teaching their children
- The elders preserving ancient memory
- The youth rising to reclaim identity
- The leaders standing in righteousness
- The watchmen sounding the walarm
- The scattered tribes awakening in every land

It is dedicated to the broken, the wounded, the lost, and the overlooked— for Yahuah has promised:
**"I will seek that which was lost,**
**and bring again that which was driven away,**
**and will bind up that which was broken,**
**and will strengthen that which was sick."**
—Ezekiel 34:16

It is dedicated to the remnant who tremble at His word, who long for the return of the divine King, who wait for the restoration of the House of David, and who will one day rejoice under the righteous leadership of the Prince whom Yahuah will raise up.

It is dedicated to those who believe that our history matters,
- our identity matters,
- our covenant matters,
- our destiny matters,
- and that Yashar'el will rise again.

Finally, this work is dedicated to every soul who has cried out in the night, seeking truth, purpose, belonging, and hope—for Yahuah has heard your cry, and He is gathering His people from the four corners of the earth. May this book strengthen your faith, illuminate your path, and remind you that you are part of the greatest restoration the world has ever known.

**To the scattered remnant returning home—
this book is for you!**

———————————————

# ACKNOWLEDGMENTS

## *Honor to yahuah, supporters,*
## *Scholars, and the remnant*

All praise, honor, and esteem belong to Yahuah Elohei Yashar'el, the One who declares the end from the beginning, the Keeper of covenant, the Restorer of truth, and the Shepherd of His people. Without His guidance, breath, wisdom, and mercy, this work could not exist. He is the Author of history, the Redeemer of the remnant, and the Giver of revelation. Everything in this book—every insight, every chapter, every line—is under His direction and for His esteem.

### 1. First and Above All—To Yahuah
I acknowledge Yahuah, the Most High, whose Spirit stirred the awakening in these last days, opening the eyes of His scattered people and calling them back to covenant. He alone is the One who:
- Preserves His word
- Reveals hidden things
- Raises up leaders in their seasons
- Unites the tribes of Yashar'el
- Restores what was lost
- Honors His promises to Abraham, Isaac, and Jacob

Every truth written in these pages flows from His breath. May His name be exalted forever.

### 2. To the Messiah, the Son of David
Honor is given to the divine Messiah, the One through whom salvation, redemption, resurrection, and eternal life are given. This work recognizes His eternal reign, His kingship over heaven and earth, and His role as the ultimate cornerstone of the restored Kingdom. Under Him, the Davidic Prince will govern in righteousness. May all Israel acknowledge the One whose reign shall never end.

### 3. To the Remnant of Yashar'el
This book is written with deep gratitude for the awakening remnant—the sons and daughters of the scattered tribes who have searched, wrestled, questioned, prayed, endured, and rediscovered the covenant of their ancestors.

Thank you—for your courage, your hunger for truth, your dedication to Torah, and your willingness to walk away from the traditions of men in order to embrace the commandments of Yahuah. Your endurance through hardship, rejection, exile, and spiritual warfare is a testimony that the hand of Yahuah is upon you. You are the living fulfillment of prophecy.

### 4. To the Scholars, Historians, and Keepers of Ancient Texts

This work would not be possible without the scholars, archivists, translators, and archaeologists who dedicated their lives to preserving and uncovering the texts of antiquity:

- The caretakers of the Dead Sea Scrolls
- The translators of the Tanakh
- The interpreters of Second Temple literature
- The historians who preserved ancient maps and records
- The researchers who traced diasporic movements

Your meticulous labor has preserved the witnesses of Scripture and ancient writings, enabling this generation to rediscover truths long buried beneath layers of time, empire, conquest, and forgetfulness.

Your work is a blessing to all who seek to understand the Kingdom of Yahuah.

### 5. To the Teachers, Elders, and Spiritual Leaders

To those who shepherd assemblies, families, and communities returning to righteousness—your devotion, patience, and commitment to truth have cultivated fertile ground for the awakening of Yashar'el. Your teachings, encouragement, and example have inspired many to pursue a deeper walk with Yahuah.

You have stood in the gap, corrected with love, labored with humility, and guided with wisdom. May Yahuah continue to strengthen your hands.

### 6. To the Builders and Lovers of Truth

To those who search the Scriptures day and night, who question everything, who test every doctrine, who refuse to be satisfied with superficial answers —your thirst for knowledge is sacred. You are the explorers of prophecy, the restorers of forgotten truths, the scribes of a new generation. Your relentless pursuit has pushed this movement forward.

## 7. To the Sufferers and the Survivors

To those who have endured:

- Captivity
- Oppression
- Displacement
- Discrimination
- Loss
- Trauma
- Erasure of identity
- Families torn apart
- Histories rewritten
- Names taken
- Roots severed

Yet still cling to hope, faith, and truth—this acknowledgment is for you. Your endurance proves the faithfulness of Yahuah. Your survival is prophecy fulfilled. Your rising is a sign that the restoration of Yashar'el is at hand.

## 8. To My Family and Loved Ones

To family, friends, supporters, and those who encouraged the vision— you are treasured. Your patience, strength, prayers, and belief in the importance of this work have made the journey possible. Your support is a blessing beyond measure.

## 9. To the Next Generation

To the youth—sons, daughters, and children of the remnant— you will inherit a world in transformation, a world entering the Kingdom age. May you:

- Walk in covenant
- Embrace your identity
- Love righteousness
- Reject the ways of darkness
- Lift up Yahuah with boldness
- Guard your heritage
- Serve your people with humility
- Look for the restoration of all things

The future of Yashar'el is in your hands.

## 10. A Final Word of Gratitude

To every reader of this book:

May Yahuah open your understanding, strengthen your heart, and guide your steps as you study these words. This work is not simply the product of research, writing, or scholarship—it is the outflow of prophecy, revelation, and the movement of Yahuah among His people.

May this book inspire you to seek Him more deeply, honor Him more faithfully, and walk in holiness as the Kingdom approaches.

---

# PREFACE

### *The awakening of a nation and the Revelation of a promise*

The journey that led to this book is not merely the exploration of ancient texts, prophetic visions, or cultural history—it is part of a much larger movement occurring across the earth. We are living in a generation unlike any before us, a generation witnessing the awakening of a scattered people, the remembrance of forgotten identities, and the unfolding of promises spoken thousands of years ago.

Across continents and islands, among diverse nations and languages, a quiet but powerful stirring is taking place. Men and women from every corner of the world are discovering truths long hidden, buried beneath layers of captivity, dispersion, colonization, and historical distortion. They are learning—some for the first time—that they are descendants of the ancient people of Yashar'el. They are returning to the covenant of their fathers, seeking Yahuah with sincerity, humility, and trembling.

This book emerges from that awakening.

## 1. The Purpose of This Work

The purpose of this book is not simply to provide information or theological commentary. Its purpose is to reveal the prophetic identity, mission, and role of the figure known in Scripture as:

- "My servant David"
- "One shepherd"
- "The Prince"
- "The Nasi"
- "The leader forever"
- "The Branch of David"
- "The Prince of the Congregation" (in the Dead Sea Scrolls)

It is intended to:

- Illuminate the prophetic timeline of the last days
- Reveal the restoration of the twelve tribes
- Explain the role of the Davidic Prince in the Millennial Kingdom
- Connect Tanakh prophecy with Second Temple literature
- Clarify the dual-messiah expectation in the Dead Sea Scrolls
- Affirm the identity and destiny of the remnant of Yashar'el today

- Strengthen the faith of those who know they are living in prophetic times

This book is not written as speculation. It is grounded in:
- Scripture
- History
- Prophetic consistency
- Israelite tradition
- Ancient commentary
- Archaeological findings
- Dead Sea Scroll scholarship
- Covenantal theology

The goal is to present **a clear, unified prophetic portrait** of the end-time Davidic Prince and the Kingdom he helps establish.

## 2. The Audience of This Book

This book is for:

### A. The awakened remnant of Yashar'el
Those who know or suspect they descend from the ancient tribes.

### B. Students of prophecy
Those who study the Tanakh to understand the end-time order.

### C. Seekers of truth
Those who long for clarity regarding Israel's future and the promises of Yahuah.

### D. Leaders and teachers
Those who shepherd communities returning to Torah, righteousness, and covenant identity.

### E. The nations who recognize Yahuah
Those who wish to understand the future Kingdom and their role within it.

### F. Future generations
Children and grandchildren who will live in the unfolding of these prophecies.

This book is especially for those who believe Yahuah is restoring the identity, purpose, and unity of His people across the globe.

## 3. Why This Message Is Needed Today

The world is entering a season of unprecedented shaking. Across the na-

tions we see:
- The collapse of political systems
- The rise of violence and injustice
- Growing deception and falsehood
- Spiritual confusion
- Division among peoples
- Displacement and diaspora communities rising
- Prophetic signs in nature, nations, and world events

Simultaneously, we see a spiritual awakening among the descendants of Yashar'el—an awakening in:
- Identity
- Torah
- Understanding
- Covenant
- Righteousness
- Prophetic clarity
- Cultural roots
- Historical memory

This dual movement—shaking and awakening—is the backdrop against-which the Davidic Prince emerges.

This book speaks into that moment, providing the prophetic framework to recognize what Yahuah is doing.

### 4. A Restoration of Truth Long Suppressed
For centuries the identity of Yashar'el and the understanding of the Davidic Prince have been suppressed or misunderstood due to:
- Diaspora
- Enslavement
- Colonization
- Destruction of records
- Forced assimilation
- Religious distortions
- Political manipulation
- The erasure of ancient cultures

But Yahuah promised:
**"I will open your graves, and cause you to come up out of your graves...and bring you into the land of Israel."**—Ezekiel 37:12

This is not merely a physical resurrection but **a cultural and spiritual resurrection.** The Prince is part of that resurrection—anointed to lead a healed nation into its prophetic destiny.

### 5. The Voice of the Prophets Still Speaks
The prophets spoke not only to their generation but to ours.
- Hosea foretold Israel's long exile and sudden awakening
- Jeremiah spoke of Jacob's Trouble and the rise of David
- Isaiah described the nations coming to Zion for Torah
- Ezekiel detailed the Temple, the tribes, and the Prince
- Zechariah described the nations celebrating Sukkot
- Daniel explained the fall of all empires and the rise of Yahuah's Kingdom
- The Dead Sea Scrolls described the Prince of the Congregation

Their messages are more relevant now than ever. This book draws from their words to assemble a complete picture.

### 6. The Davidic Prince: A Message for the Last Days
We live in the generation where:
- Identity is returning
- Truth is resurfacing
- Lies are crumbling
- Nations are shaking
- Prophecies are aligning
- The remnant is awakening

This is the generation that will witness:
- The return of the tribes
- The rebuilding of the Temple
- The Covenant of Peace
- The defeat of rebellious nations
- The restoration of David's throne
- The reign of the divine Messiah
- The rise of the Davidic Prince

This book is written for that generation—**our generation.**

### 7. A Word to the Reader
As you read this book, may you:
- Be strengthened in your identity
- Be encouraged in your calling

14

- Be awakened to truth
- Be filled with hope
- Be established in righteousness
- Be aligned with the will of Yahuah
- Be prepared for the days ahead

This is not a time for fear, confusion, or despair. It is a time for clarity, obedience, courage, and faith. The same Yahuah who brought our ancestors out of Egypt will bring us out of the nations. The same Yahuah who promised a kingdom in the days of David will restore that kingdom in our time. The same Yahuah who spoke through the prophets is speaking still. And the same Yahuah who promised a Prince for the end days will raise him up when the appointed time comes.

### 8. The Journey Ahead

This book is not the end of the story. It is a beginning—a step on the path toward:

- Deeper understanding
- Stronger faith
- National unity
- Covenant renewal
- Righteous leadership
- The Kingdom to come

As we move forward, let every reader remember:

- **Yahuah is restoring His people.**
- **Yahuah is preparing His Kingdom.**
- **Yahuah is faithful to His promises.**
- **Yahuah is raising up His Prince.**
- **Yahuah is gathering the tribes.**
- **Yahuah is returning to Zion.**

May this work serve as a lamp for your feet and a guide for your understanding as you witness the greatest restoration in human history.

---

# AUTHOR'S NOTE

### *A Personal Word to the Reader*

This book was not written from a place of academic distance, nor from the safety of detached scholarship. It was written from the depths of a spiritual awakening—one rooted in Scripture, guided by the Spirit of Yahuah, and shaped by the lived experiences of a scattered people returning to their identity.

As I studied the prophets, traced the lineage of the House of David, analyzed the Dead Sea Scrolls, and followed the threads of restoration throughout the Tanakh, one truth became undeniable: **Yahuah is awakening His people in these last days.** This awakening is not metaphorical. It is not symbolic. It is happening around us—and within us.

For many of us, the journey back to identity has been long, painful, and personal. We carry the memories of ancestors taken into captivity, families broken by oppression, names stripped away, cultures erased, and histories rewritten. Yet the Most High has not forgotten us. Though our people were scattered to the four corners of the earth, He preserved our spirit. He preserved our story. He preserved our destiny.This book is part of that preservation.

## 1. A Message That Found Me Before I Found It

I did not set out with the intention of writing a book about the Davidic Prince. In truth, the subject found me. Time and again, as I studied Scripture, the same theme reappeared:

- A ruler
- A shepherd
- A servant
- A son of David
- A leader of the restored tribes
- A prince under the reign of the divine Messiah
- A man anointed in the last days for the people of Yashar'el

The more I researched, the clearer the picture became. The Prince is not a symbolic figure. He is not an allegory. He is a literal ruler who arises during the restoration of Yashar'el—and his role is central to the prophetic future. This book is a response to that revelation.

## 2. Written for the Awakening Remnant

This work is written for those who:

- Feel the stirring in their spirit
- Sense the call of identity
- Know they are part of something ancient
- Recognize the times in which we live
- Are returning to Torah after generations of forgetting
- Have endured hardship yet still believe
- Are hungry for truth beyond tradition
- Understand that prophecy is unfolding in real time

This book is for the sons and daughters of Yashar'el who know that the Most High is gathering His people again.

## 3. A Work Rooted in Study, Prayer, and Revelation

This book is not the product of one discipline but many:

- Scriptural exegesis
- Historical analysis
- Cultural memory
- Archaeological evidence
- Dead Sea Scroll insights
- Pseudepigraphal comparisons
- Linguistic study
- Prayer
- Fasting
- Meditation
- Revelation from the Ruach HaQodesh

Every chapter was written slowly, deliberately, and with reverence for the Most High and His word. I approached this work not as a scholar seeking recognition but as a servant seeking truth.

## 4. Why This Topic Is Critically Important

Understanding the Davidic Prince clarifies:

- The structure of the Millennial Kingdom
- The restoration of the twelve tribes
- The prophetic timeline of the last days
- The expectations of the remnant
- The relationship between Messiah and the Prince
- The importance of the Temple vision in Ezekiel
- The identity of Yashar'el in the nations
- The coming unification of Judah and Ephraim

- The role of Yahuah's covenant with David
- The destiny of the scattered people in this generation

The Prince stands as a bridge between the scattered past and the restored future. To understand him is to understand the Kingdom.

## 5. A Journey for the Reader

As you engage with the pages that follow, I encourage you to:
- Search the Scriptures for yourself
- Test everything
- Pray for understanding
- Seek the guidance of the Ruach HaQodesh
- Read slowly and thoughtfully
- Consider how prophecy speaks to our time
- Recognize yourself, your family, and your story within the restoration narrative

This book is an invitation to deeper study and greater awakening.

## 6. A Final Word from the Author

We are living in the days our ancestors longed to see.

We are the generation witnessing the beginning of the end—the end of exile, the end of confusion, the end of captivity. We are the generation that will see the rise of the Prince, the rebuilding of the Temple, the return of Yahuah's presence, and the restoration of the Kingdom. The world may tremble, but Yahuah's people will stand.
- Prophecy is unfolding.
- Identity is returning.
- Truth is rising.
- The covenant is awakening.
- The Kingdom is at hand.

I pray that this book strengthens your understanding, deepens your faith, and prepares your heart for the days ahead.

May Yahuah guide you.

May His wisdom rest upon you.

May His Spirit lead you into all truth.

**May the awakening of Yashar'el continue—until the Prince rises, the tribes return, and Yahuah dwells among His people forever.**

---

# FOREWORD

## *A Word Before the Journey Begins*

There are moments in history when the voice of the Most High breaks through the noise of nations and the confusion of men. Moments when prophecy, long dormant, begins to stir. Moments when the scattered seeds of an ancient people awaken beneath the weight of centuries and rise again toward the light. We are living in such a moment. For generations, the identity, purpose, and destiny of Yashar'el lay buried beneath captivity, oppression, dispersions, invasions, slavery, colonization, and centuries of historical erasure. Yet Yahuah, who neither sleeps nor slumbers, has never forgotten His people. He made an everlasting covenant with Abraham, Isaac, and Jacob, and He swore to restore their descendants —not spiritually only, but historically, culturally, tribally, and nationally.

Now, in these last days, a great awakening is underway. Men and women on every continent—across Africa, the Americas, the islands, the Middle East, Europe, and throughout the world—are remembering who they are. They are returning to Torah. They are reclaiming covenant identity. They are reading the Scriptures with awakened eyes and renewed understanding. They are hearing the call of Yahuah echo across generations:
**"Return unto Me, and I will return unto you."**

It is into this moment of restoration that this book arrives.

## 1. A Timely Work for a Prophetic Generation

The subject of the Davidic Prince has long been either misunderstood, overlooked, or misinterpreted. For centuries, religious traditions blurred the distinction between the divine Messiah and the mortal ruler described in Ezekiel, Hosea, Jeremiah, and the writings found among the Dead Sea Scrolls. This book restores that distinction with clarity, scholarship, and spiritual insight.

It presents the Scriptures as they were given:
with a divine, eternal King— and a human, earthly Prince raised up in the last days to shepherd Yashar'el under the authority of Yahuah.

- This is not speculation.
- This is not tradition.
- This is prophecy.
- The prophets spoke of him.

19

- The Psalms anticipated him.
- Ezekiel described his duties in detail.
- Hosea foresaw his timing.
- Jeremiah revealed his mission.
- Isaiah hinted at his role in the restored kingdom.
- The Dead Sea Scrolls confirmed the expectation of a Davidic leader in the final age.

This book brings all these threads together.

## 2. A Work of Restoration, Identity, and Awakening

The restoration of the House of David cannot be understood apart from the restoration of the House of Yashar'el. For the Prince cannot rise until the people awaken.

- He cannot lead until the nation returns.
- He cannot shepherd until the flock gathers.
- He cannot unify until the tribes remember who they are.
- And he cannot be recognized until Yashar'el is spiritually prepared to receive him.

The author of this work writes not from the outside looking in—but from within the awakening itself. This book was written by someone who understands the journey, the struggle, the questions, the longing, and the identity rediscovered by so many in this generation. That authenticity echoes through every chapter.

## 3. A Bridge Between the Ancient and the Present

One of the strengths of this work is its commitment to both ancient sources and modern awakening. It bridges:

- The Tanakh
- The prophetic writings
- The Apocrypha
- The Pseudepigrapha
- The Dead Sea Scrolls
- The history of the diaspora
- The awakening of the remnant
- The future restoration of the Kingdom

This is the kind of scholarship that honors the past while speaking directly to the present moment and preparing the reader for the prophetic future.

## 4. A Message for the Humble and the Faithful
This book is not for the proud, the hardened, or the dismissive.
It is for the seekers.
- The broken.
- The hungry.
- The awakened.

Those who know there is more to the story of Scripture than tradition ever taught them. If you are one who senses something stirring in the spirit—something ancient, something prophetic, something true—then this book is for you. If you are one who feels drawn to the identity of Yashar'el—to Torah, covenant, righteousness, and the promises of the prophets— then this book will strengthen your journey.

If you are one who wants to understand the role of the Davidic Prince— his identity, mission, authority, character, and place in the Kingdom—this book will give you clarity.

## 5. A Word of Encouragement
As you read, do so with:
- An open heart
- A discerning mind
- A love for truth
- A respect for Scripture
- A desire to walk in righteousness

Allow the Ruach HaQodesh to guide your understanding. Allow the prophets to speak for themselves. Allow the Most High to reveal what has been hidden. The days ahead will require clarity, strength, and wisdom. This book provides tools for all three.

## 6. A Final Blessing Before You Begin
May Yahuah open your eyes to the words of the prophets. May He strengthen your identity as a descendant of Yashar'el. May He prepare your heart for the restoration of His Kingdom. May He guide you in understanding the role of the Prince He will raise up. May He lead you into all truth as the days of redemption unfold. May He establish you among the remnant who keep His commands and hold fast to His covenant.

The journey before you is sacred. Turn the page—and enter the unfolding plan of Yahuah for His people.

# INTRODUCTION

*The return of prophecy and*
*The age of restoration*

The subject of the Davidic Prince—the mortal ruler whom Yahuah raises up in the last days—has long been overshadowed by confusion, tradition, and incomplete teaching. While the divine Messiah reigns forever as King, Scripture also reveals a human ruler, a son of David, who shepherds the restored nation of Yashar'el during the Millennial Kingdom. For generations, this figure has remained misunderstood, often blended together with Messiah Himself, or dismissed as a metaphor. Yet the prophets speak of him with clarity, specificity, and striking consistency.

This book seeks to unveil that truth fully, faithfully, and without compromise. The return of the Davidic Prince is not merely a theological concept; it is a prophetic certainty woven into the fabric of Scripture—from Hosea to Ezekiel, from Isaiah to Jeremiah, from the Psalms to the Dead Sea Scrolls. His rise is inseparable from the restoration of the twelve tribes, the rebuilding of the Temple, the reunification of Yashar'el, and the establishment of the Kingdom of Yahuah upon the earth. This Introduction sets the stage for that revelation.

## 1. Why This Book Matters Now

We are living in a time when prophecy once dismissed as symbolic is manifesting before our eyes. Identity is returning to a scattered people. Ancient truths buried by empire, captivity, and colonization are resurfacing. The Scriptures speak of a generation that:

- Returns to Torah
- Remembers who they are
- Walks in covenant
- Repents with sincerity
- Seeks Yahuah wholeheartedly
- Awakens after centuries of silence
- Hears the voice of the prophets anew

That generation is now. This awakening is not random, cultural, or social—it is spiritual. It is the fulfillment of the prophetic words:

**"Afterward shall the children of Yashar'el return, and seek Yahuah their Elohim, and David their king..."** —Hosea 3:5

When Yashar'el awakens, the Prince must arise.

22

## 2. The Forgotten Prophecy of the Davidic Prince

For centuries, the focus of biblical prophecy was narrowed almost exclusively to Messiah's return. While this is undeniably central, it overshadowed a parallel truth: **Yahuah appoints a mortal ruler—the Prince—during the Millennial Kingdom.** Ezekiel devotes nine full chapters to the Prince's responsibilities, inheritance, offerings, authority, and relationship to the Temple. Jeremiah speaks of him. Hosea prophesies his appearance. Isaiah hints at his role beneath the reign of Messiah. The Psalms describe the restoration of David's line. The Dead Sea Scrolls confirm Israelite expectation of:

- A priestly Messiah (of Aaron)
- A royal messiah/prince (of David)

Two distinct figures. This book restores the clarity that the prophets preserved.

## 3. What This Book Covers

This work is not a shallow overview; it is a comprehensive prophetic investigation supported by Scripture, Second Temple literature, and historical context. This book covers:

### A. Scriptural foundations of the Davidic Prince
Hosea 3 • Jeremiah 30 • Ezekiel 34 • Ezekiel 37 • Ezekiel 40–48 • Isaiah 11 • Micah 5 • Zechariah

### B. His role in the Millennial Kingdom
Temple governance • offerings • justice • tribal land distribution • Feast observances

### C. His identity as "My Servant David"
A mortal ruler, not the Messiah Himself

### D. The dual-messiah expectation in the Dead Sea Scrolls
Prince of the Congregation • Branch of David • Messiah of Israel

### E. The restoration of the twelve tribes of Yashar'el
Tribal unity • diaspora ingathering • Ezekiel's two sticks

### F. The Prince's relationship to Messiah
A vice-regent under the eternal King

### G. The Prince's character, humility, and calling
A shepherd-king like the first David

### H. Signs of his appearance in the last days
Awakening • repentance • national unity • Temple reconstruction

### I. The global transformation in the Kingdom Age
Nations coming to Jerusalem • Torah going forth from Zion

### J. The purpose of the Prince in Yahuah's eternal plan
Unity, justice, restoration, peace, and holiness

This book is built upon Scripture and supported by ancient Israelite texts.

### 4. The Israelite Perspective of the Last Days
Much of Western theology has interpreted end-time prophecy through a Gentile or European lens. This book restores the original perspective: prophecy is Israelite. It speaks of:
- Israelite land
- Israelite covenant
- Israelite tribes
- Israelite leadership
- Israelite identity
- Israelite governance
- Israelite restoration

The prophets did not address Rome, Paris, London, or Washington. They addressed:
- Jerusalem
- Zion
- The mountains of Yashar'el
- The scattered descendants of Jacob
- The nations surrounding Israel
- The future Kingdom centered in the land promised to Abraham

To understand prophecy, one must return to the context of the people to whom it was given.

### 5. The Importance of the Prince in Prophetic Fulfillment
The Prince's role is essential because he is:
- The earthly ruler of the reunited nation
- The administrator of justice

- The guardian of the land
- The overseer of the Temple
- The representative of the people
- The restorer of tribal boundaries
- The protector against oppression
- The shepherd who guides the nation in righteousness

He stands at the intersection of:

- Covenant
- Kingship
- Temple worship
- National unity
- Tribal inheritance
- International order
- Divine presence
- Israelite identity

Without the Prince, the Millennial Kingdom would lack its earthly structure.

## 6. The Dead Sea Scrolls: Confirming the Ancient Expectation

The Dead Sea Scrolls do not contradict Scripture— they confirm it.
The Qumran community expected:

- **A priestly Messiah of Aaron**
- **A royal messiah/prince of David**
- A final war
- A restored Temple
- A purified people
- A Davidic ruler governing in righteousness
- A priestly leader guiding in holiness

Their writings illuminate the Israelite understanding of messianic prophecy during the Second Temple period. This book integrates these texts with Scripture for a complete prophetic picture.

## 7. The Rise of the Remnant: The Key to Understanding the Prince

The Prince does not arise in a vacuum.
He emerges when the people:

- Are humbled
- Are scattered
- Are oppressed
- Are awakened
- Return to Torah

- Cry out to Yahuah
- Recognize their need for righteous leadership
- Long for covenant restoration

The remnant is the soil from which the Prince rises. His emergence is the answer to their prayers.

## 8. A Word on Identity and Calling

This book embraces the truth that many descendants of the ancient Israelites have been scattered to:

- Africa
- The Americas
- The Caribbean
- Europe
- The Middle East
- Asia
- The islands of the sea

Their identity was stolen, but their calling never changed. The prophecy of awakening is fulfilled in them. And the role of the Prince is intertwined with the return of the people to their rightful identity and inheritance.

## 9. A Call to Read with Understanding

As you open the pages of this book, approach the journey with:

- An open heart
- A discerning spirit
- A desire for truth
- A willingness to unlearn falsehood
- A commitment to study the Scriptures deeply
- A readiness to accept what Yahuah reveals
- A sensitivity to the leading of the Ruach HaQodesh

This work is not about modern politics, denominations, or traditions. It is about the **Kingdom**, the **covenant,** the **prophets**, and **the restoration of Yashar'el.**

## 10. The Journey Ahead

The chapters that follow will guide you through:

- The prophetic foundation of the Prince
- The role he plays in the end times
- The structure of the Millennial Kingdom
- The Temple ordinances
- The restoration of the tribes

- The identity of the remnant
- The purpose of the Davidic line
- The transformation of the nations
- The glory of Yahuah returning to Zion

By the end of this book, you will see the entire prophetic landscape with new clarity.

- You will understand why Yahuah reserved this message for the last generation.
- You will recognize the threads of prophecy coming together.
- You will perceive the hand of Yahuah in world events.
- You will be prepared to witness the restoration of all things.

This is more than an introduction— it is an invitation into the unfolding plan of Yahuah for His people.

- The Kingdom is returning.
- The tribes are awakening.
- The stage is set.
- The Prince will rise.

Yahuah will dwell among His people.

Let us begin.

———————————

# CHAPTER ONE

## THE DAVIDIC COVENANT
## AND ITS ETERNAL PROMISE

The study of the end-time Davidic Prince cannot begin with Ezekiel, Hosea, or Jeremiah. It must begin at the root, with the covenant Yahuah established with David—the man after His own heart. This covenant, recorded in **2 Samuel 7**, reiterated in **1 Chronicles 17**, and exalted in **Psalm 89**, is one of the most foundational covenants in all Scripture. It shapes the identity of Yashar'el, anchors the promise of restoration, and establishes the expectation that a descendant of David will rise again in the latter days.

This covenant is the backbone of all prophetic references to "David My servant" in Hosea 3, Jeremiah 30, Ezekiel 34, Ezekiel 37, and Ezekiel 40 48. Without the Davidic Covenant, the end-time role of the Prince makes no theological sense. With it, the entire prophetic picture becomes clear.

Furthermore, the **Dead Sea Scrolls (DSS)**—the writings of an ancient Israelite sect at Qumran—demonstrate that Israelites before the 1st century deeply believed the Davidic Covenant required:
- A future, human Davidic ruler
- A military and governmental leader
- A figure called the **Prince of the Congregation**
- One who would arise in **the last days**
- Distinct from the priestly and divine Messianic figure

This chapter lays the foundation for everything that follows by exploring:
1. The Eternal Covenant With David
2. The Collapse of the Monarchy and the Prophetic Tension
3. Why the Covenant Requires a Future Human Ruler
4. The Distinction Between the Divine Messiah and the Davidic Prince
5. How the Dead Sea Scrolls Interpreted the Davidic Covenant
6. DSS Passages About the "Prince of the Congregation"
7. How DSS and Ezekiel align perfectly
8. The prophetic logic that demands David's throne rise again
Let us begin where Scripture begins.

## 1. The Birth of the Davidic Covenant: 2 Samuel 7
The covenant begins with David's desire to build Yahuah a permanent dwelling place. Instead, Yahuah reverses the initiative—David will not build a house for Yahuah; rather, **Yahuah will build a house for David. 2 Samuel 7:12–16 (KJV)**

12 …I will set up thy seed after thee…

13 He shall build an house for my name, and I will establish the throne of his kingdom for ever.

16 And thine house and thy kingdom shall be established for ever before thee: thy throne shall be established for ever.

Three eternal promises are stated:

1. **A HOUSE — a perpetual dynasty**
2. **A THRONE — perpetual royal authority**
3. **A KINGDOM — a perpetual national reign over Yashar'el**

None of these are temporary. None are symbolic. None are transferable to another family. This covenant is permanent and irrevocable.

### 2. The Covenant Reaffirmed After the Exile: 1 Chronicles 17

After the Babylonian captivity, when no king sat on the throne, 1 Chronicles restates the exact same covenant. This is proof that exile did not nullify it.

**1 Chronicles 17:14**

*"I will settle him in mine house and in my kingdom for ever: and his throne shall be established for evermore."*

Key points:

- The covenant survived the exile
- David's line remained chosen
- The throne remained promised
- The restoration remained future

The covenant is eternal because it is based on Yahuah's holiness, not Israel's performance.

### 3. The Covenant Intensified: Psalm 89

Psalm 89 is the covenant's legal commentary. It converts the simple promises of 2 Samuel 7 into a sworn divine oath.

**Psalm 89:34–36**

*34 My covenant will I not break…*

*35 Once have I sworn by my holiness that I will not lie unto David.*

*36 His seed shall endure for ever…*

And:

**Psalm 89:37**

*It shall be established for ever as the moon…*

The Davidic promise is compared to:

- The moon
- The witness in the sky
- A permanent heavenly ordinance

This covenant is **unbreakable.**

## 4. The Collapse of the Monarchy Creates a Prophetic Crisis

By the fall of Jerusalem in 586 BCE:

- The Temple was destroyed
- The throne was empty
- The Davidic monarchy was gone
- The people were scattered
- The nation was exiled

It appeared the covenant had failed. But the prophets refused to accept this idea. Instead, they prophesied a **future restoration.**

**They did *not* say:**

- *"David's line has ended."*
- *"The covenant is cancelled."*
- *"There will be no more Davidic ruler."*

**They *did* say:**

- *David will return*
- *A Davidic ruler will arise*
- *He will rule the twelve tribes*
- *He will be prince forever*
- *He will shepherd Yashar'el*
- *He will govern the Millennial Kingdom*

Thus, the collapse of the monarchy ignited the prophetic hope.

## 5. Why the Covenant Requires a Future Human Davidic Ruler

The text of Scripture requires it:

### A. "Thy seed" = physical offspring

Hebrew: זרע (zera)

Not symbolic. Not spiritualized.

### B. "His throne shall be established forever"

- Requires a throne.
- Requires a ruler.
- Requires restoration.

## C. David's kingdom is earthly, not only heavenly

The Davidic Prince rules the **land. D. Ezekiel's Prince is mortal**. Because he:

- Offers sin offerings (Ezek. 45:22)
- Has sons who inherit land (Ezek. 46:16)
- Is assigned territory between Judah and Benjamin (Ezek. 48:21–22)
- Enters and exits the Temple by ordinance
- Submits to priests (sons of Zadok)

Mashiach cannot be this man.

## E. The covenant logically demands a restoration

If the throne fell, it must rise again. Prophetically:

- The dry bones rise (Ezek. 37:11–14)
- The two sticks unite (37:15–22)
- David returns as leader (37:24–25)
- The covenant of peace is given (37:26)
- Yahuah's presence returns (43:1–7)
- The Prince rules in the restored Temple (40–48)

The covenant sets all of this in motion.

## 6. The Dead Sea Scrolls: The Ancient Israelite Interpretation of the Covenant

The Dead Sea Scrolls (DSS), written by an Israelite sect living near Qumran, contain the earliest surviving interpretations of the Davidic Covenant outside the Tanakh. Crucially, these Israelite writings expected:

- A **future Davidic ruler**
- A **war-leader**
- A figure called the **Prince of the Congregation**
- Connected to the **Branch of David** prophecies
- Appearing in **the last days**
- Distinct from the priestly Messiah
- Ruling beside a priestly leader
- Governing the tribes of Israel

These expectations mirror Ezekiel's portrait of the Prince. Let us examine the key scrolls.

## 7. DSS Witness 1 — 1QM (War Scroll): "Prince of the Congregation"

The War Scroll describes the final eschatological battle between:

- Sons of Light (righteous Israelites)

- Sons of Darkness (enemy nations)

Throughout this scroll, a specific leader appears:
- נשיא העדה — Nasi ha-Edah
- **Prince of the Congregation**
- **A Davidic military ruler**

**1QM 5:1–2**

*"This shall be the rule for the **Prince of the Congregation** when he musters the men for battle…"*

**1QM 7:5–6**

*"The Priest shall walk before them… and the **Prince of the Congregation** shall strengthen them."*

This reflects two roles:
- The **Priestly Messiah** leads spiritually
- The **Davidic Prince** leads militarily

Exactly the model described in Ezekiel.

**1QM 17:5–9**

*"You, the God of Israel, shall empower the **Prince of the Congregation,** appointing him **over all the leaders of the tribes of Israel…**"*

This is overwhelmingly significant:
- The Prince is **appointed by Yahuah**
- He stands **over the tribal chiefs**
- He rules a restored Israel
- This is Ezekiel 48's tribal order

## 8. DSS Witness 2 — 4Q285 ("Branch of David Text")

**4Q285, Fragment 5**

*"The **Branch of David** will rise… and the **Prince of the Congregation** will put to death the leader of the Kittim…"*

This fragment identifies:
- **Branch of David** = Davidic ruler
- **Prince of the Congregation** = same or connected role

Thus the DSS directly link the Prince with David's lineage.

### 9. DSS Witness 3 — 4Q161 (Isaiah Pesher)

Commentary on Isaiah 11:1 ("A Branch shall arise from Jesse")

**4Q161 Fragment 8–10**

*"...this refers to the **Branch of David**, who will arise in the last days to deliver Israel."*

This shows:

- Last-days fulfillment
- Davidic identity
- Warrior deliverer

### 10. DSS Witness 4 — 4Q174 (Florilegium)

A midrash on 2 Samuel 7 and Amos 9:11.

**4Q174 Column 1**

*"...this refers to the Branch of David, who will arise with the Interpreter of the Law in the last days."*

Two figures:

- **Branch of David** → Davidic ruler
- **Interpreter of the Law** → Priestly Messiah

The Two-Leader Model reflects Ezekiel 40–48.

### 11. DSS Witness 5 — 1QS (Community Rule)

**1QS IX, 11**

*"...until the coming of the **Messiahs of Aaron and Israel**."*

In DSS terminology:

- "Messiah of Aaron" = Priestly Messiah
- "Messiah of Israel" = Davidic Prince

This is identical to Ezekiel:

- Priests (sons of Zadok)
- Prince (line of David)

### 12. DSS Witness 6 — 4Q252 (Genesis Commentary)

**4Q252 Fragment 1, Column 5**

*"...until the coming of the Messiah of Righteousness, the Branch of David."*

Again, Davidic. Again, future. Again, last days.

### 13. How DSS Interpretation Confirms the Davidic Covenant

The Dead Sea Scrolls show that ancient Israelites believed:

- The Davidic Covenant was not fulfilled in ancient times
- It required an eschatological (end-time) fulfillment

- A human Davidic ruler would emerge
- He would govern Yashar'el
- He would fight in the final war
- He would be distinct from the Priestly Messiah
- He would rule under Yahuah's authority
- He would lead the tribes in the restored kingdom

This is precisely what Ezekiel describes.

## 14. Integration: Davidic Covenant + DSS + Ezekiel

| Davidic Covenant | Dead Sea Scrolls | Ezekiel |
|---|---|---|
| Eternal dynasty | Branch of David | David My servant |
| Future ruler | Prince of the Congregation | The Prince (ha-Nasi) |
| Governance of Yashar'el | Leader of the tribes | Prince over them forever |
| Restoration | Last-days war & victory | Dry bones rise; two sticks unite |
| Kingdom | Sons of Light triumph | Israel restored to land |
| Priestly connection | Priestly Messiah with Davidic Messiah | Sons of Zadok + Prince |

## 15. Summary of Chapter One

- The Davidic Covenant guarantees a future Davidic ruler.
- This ruler is not Mashiach Yahusha, but a human descendant of David.
- The collapse of the monarchy created a prophetic expectation of future restoration.
- Ezekiel describes this ruler as the Prince (ha-Nasi).
- The Dead Sea Scrolls describe him as the Prince of the Congregation and the Branch of David.
- DSS writings confirm Israelite belief in two Messianic figures:
    - A Priestly Messiah
    - A Davidic Prince
- Both the Tanakh and DSS testify that a human Davidic ruler will govern Yashar'el in the last days.
- This chapter establishes the covenantal and historical foundation for all later chapters.

CHAPTER TWO

# THE EXILE AND THE PROMISE
# OF RESTORATION

The Davidic Covenant stands as the foundation of Israel's royal theology. Yet shortly after that covenant was given, catastrophe struck. The twelve tribes were scattered, the monarchy collapsed, the Temple was destroyed, and the land was left desolate. What followed was the most traumatic national event in Israelite history: **the exile.**

To understand the emergence of the latter-day Davidic Prince, we must understand the exile and the prophetic promise of restoration. The prophets did not treat exile as the end of Israel's story—rather, exile became the stage upon which Yahuah would reveal His covenantal faithfulness, His redemptive power, and His future plan to restore all twelve tribes under the rule of a Davidic shepherd.

This chapter examines:
1. Moses' prophetic warning of exile
2. The scattering of both houses of Israel
3. The collapse of the Davidic monarchy
4. The prophetic expectation that followed
5. Why restoration required a Davidic ruler
6. The timeline of regathering in the latter days
7. Prophetic clues for understanding the Davidic Prince
8. The Dead Sea Scrolls' interpretation of the exile
9. The emergence of end-time restoration theology

**1. Moses Foretold the Exile Long Before It Happened**
The exile did not catch Yahuah by surprise. Centuries before it occurred, Moses prophesied it with stunning detail. The Torah teaches that Israel's occupation of the land was conditional upon obedience to the covenant, but the identity of Israel and the Davidic Covenant were not conditional.

In the Song of Moses, and throughout Deuteronomy, Moses warns:

**Deuteronomy 28:64 (KJV)**
*"And Yahuah shall scatter thee among all people, from the one end of the earth even unto the other…"*

**Deuteronomy 30:1–3 (KJV)**
*"1 And it shall come to pass… when all these things come upon thee…*
*3 That then Yahuah thy Elohim will turn thy captivity… and will return and gather thee from all nations…"*

Three facts emerge:
- **Exile was prophesied from the beginning**
- **Regathering was also prophesied**
- **Yahuah Himself would initiate the restoration**

Thus the exile was not the termination of Israel's destiny—it was a stage in the covenantal plan.

## 2. The Division of the Kingdom and the Scattering of the Tribes

After Solomon's reign, the kingdom split:
- **Northern Kingdom (Israel / Ephraim)**
- **Southern Kingdom (Judah)**

This division is essential for end-time prophecy.

### 2.1 The Northern Tribes Scattered by Assyria (722 BCE)

The Northern Tribes—including:
- Reuben
- Gad
- Asher
- Naphtali
- Dan
- Issachar
- Zebulun
- Ephraim
- Manasseh

were carried into exile by Assyria.

These tribes disappeared from the land and became known as:
- **The Lost Tribes of Israel**
- **The House of Ephraim**

They were scattered across:
- Africa
- Asia
- Arabia
- India
- Europe

and later far beyond.

### 2.2 The Southern Kingdom Taken by Babylon (586 BCE)

Judah, Levi, and Benjamin were exiled to Babylon. Together, both exiles fulfilled the curse Moses warned about.

### 3. The Collapse of the Davidic Monarchy

The destruction of Jerusalem in 586 BCE resulted in:

- The end of the throne of David
- The captivity of the Davidic king (Zedekiah)
- No successor on the throne
- The cessation of sacrifices
- The absence of the Shekinah (glory)
- Total national ruin

This appeared to nullify the Davidic Covenant. However—the prophets refused to accept that conclusion. Why?

Because the Davidic Covenant is unconditional. Thus the collapse created a prophetic problem: If the throne fell, how will it rise again?

This problem becomes the driving force behind Israelite eschatology.

### 4. The Prophets Declare That Exile Is Not the End

When the prophets saw Israel scattered, they did not say:

- "The covenant is over."
- "The throne has ended."
- "Israel will not return."

Instead, they prophesied:

**Israel will return.**

The covenant will stand. David will reign again. Let us examine key prophecies.

### 5. Hosea: Israel Without a King —Then David Returns

The prophet Hosea speaks directly to the exile of the Northern Tribes:

**Hosea 3:4–5 (KJV)**

*"4 For the children of Israel shall abide many days without a king, and without a prince…*
*5 Afterward shall the children of Israel return, and seek Yahuah their Elohim, and David their king… in the latter days."*

This prophecy contains the formula for the entire end-time narrative:

- **Many days without a king or prince** → the exile
- **Return to the land** → the regathering
- **Seeking Yahuah** → national repentance
- **Seeking David their king** → a restored Davidic ruler in the latter days

Hosea is explicit:
- David returns
- In the last days
- As king over restored Israel

This cannot refer to ancient David, who died; nor to Mashiach Yahusha, who is not called *"a prince among them"* (Ezek. 34:24).
It refers to the Davidic Prince.

## 6. Jeremiah: After Jacob's Trouble Comes David
Jeremiah details the greatest tribulation Israel will ever face:

**Jeremiah 30:7 (KJV)**
*"Alas! for that day is great, so that none is like it: it is even the time of Jacob's trouble..."*

Immediately afterward:
**Jeremiah 30:9 (KJV)**
*"They shall serve Yahuah their Elohim, and David their king, whom I will raise up unto them."*
The order is:
- Jacob's Trouble
- Deliverance
- Restoration
- David restored as king

Jeremiah foretells a future Davidic ruler **after** the final tribulation.

## 7. Ezekiel: Restoration Requires a Davidic Shepherd
Ezekiel prophesied both the Northern and Southern tribes uniting.

**Ezekiel 34:23–24 (KJV)**
*"23 And I will set up one shepherd over them... even my servant David. 24 ...and my servant David a prince among them."*

This passage:
- Names him **David**
- Calls him **shepherd**
- Calls him **prince**
- Places him **after** the return of the flock
- Distinguishes him from Yahuah

This Davidic ruler is a human leader.

**Ezekiel 37:24–25 (KJV)**
*"24 And David my servant shall be king over them…*
*25 …and my servant David shall be their prince for ever."*

Ezekiel confirms:
- David = king
- David = prince
- His rule = forever
- Over reunited tribes

This only works with a **resurrected David** or a **Davidic descendant**. The prophets treat him as the latter: an heir who restores David's earthly throne.

### 8. The Timeline of End-Time Restoration
Combining these texts yields a clear sequence:

### 1. Scattering of all twelve tribes
(Hosea 3:4; Ezek. 37:11)

### 2. Long period "without a king, without a prince"
(Hosea 3:4)

### 3. Awakening and repentance
(Hosea 3:5)

### 4. Jacob's Trouble / Final Tribulation
(Jer. 30:7)

### 5. Deliverance by Yahuah
(Jer. 30:8)

### 6. Return to the land
(Ezek. 36:24; 37:21)

### 7. Reunification of Judah and Ephraim
(Ezek. 37:15–22)

### 8. Appointment of David as king and prince forever
(Ezek. 37:24–25)

### 9. Yahuah's glory returns to the Temple
(Ezek. 43:1–7)

### 10. The Prince begins his duties in the Millennial Temple
(Ezek. 44–48)

This timeline is foundational for understanding all future chapters.

### 9. Why Restoration Requires a Davidic Ruler
Prophets are unanimous:
- Israel cannot be restored without a Davidic leader
- The covenant throne must be reinstated
- The tribes must be governed by Yahuah's chosen ruler
- National unity requires a shepherd-king
- Worship structure requires the Prince

Thus, the covenant restoration is:

**Political — a kingdom**
**Spiritual — Yahuah's presence returns**
**Geographical — land allotments restored**
**Tribal — boundaries of the twelve tribes redrawn**
**Administrative — the Prince governs Israel**
**Priestly — sons of Zadok minister in the sanctuary**

This is why Ezekiel's final prophecy (chapters 40–48) describes:
- A new Temple
- A new priesthood order
- A new prince
- A new tribal map
- A new covenant era

The exile destroyed everything—but the restoration rebuilds everything.

### 10. The Dead Sea Scrolls on Exile and Restoration
The Dead Sea Scrolls contain some of the earliest Israelite commentary on the meaning of exile. The Qumran community believed:
- They were living in the darkness of exile
- The priesthood in Jerusalem was corrupted
- The monarchy had failed
- Israel was waiting for two Messianic figures:
    1. **A Priest-Messiah** (Messiah of Aaron)
    2. **A Davidic Prince** (Messiah of Israel / Prince of the Congregation)

- The restoration would occur in the last days
- A Davidic ruler would lead the final war and govern the tribes

This perfectly aligns with the prophetic timeline above.

### DSS Interpretation Summary
1. Exile = Israel's covenant discipline
2. The restoration = for the faithful remnant
3. The Davidic Prince = ruler of the restored nation
4. The Priestly Messiah = sanctifier of the people
5. The final war = victory of Yahuah over the nations
6. The two Messiahs work together
7. The covenant promises are fulfilled literally

The DSS confirm that ancient Israelites viewed the exile as a temporary state preceding triumph.

## 11. DSS Passages Connecting Exile to the Davidic Prince
The War Scroll (1QM) assumes Israel is in exile and waiting for divine deliverance. In that setting:

### 1QM 17:5–9
*"...You, the God of Israel, shall empower the **Prince of the Congregation,** appointing him over the leaders of the tribes..."*

This passage implies:
- A future restoration
- Tribal structure reestablished
- A Davidic ruler appointed by Yahuah

Exactly as Ezekiel 37 describes.
**4Q174 (Florilegium) also interprets 2 Samuel 7 as future:**
*"...the **Branch of David** will arise in the last days..."*
Thus the exile had not nullifi ed the covenant.

## 12. Exile as the Necessary Setup for the Prince
Without the exile:
- There would be no need for a shepherd to gather scattered sheep
- There would be no need for tribal reunification
- There would be no need for a covenant of peace
- There would be no "latter days" return to Yahuah
- There would be no restoration kingdom

- The Prince would have no people to lead

The exile creates the prophetic vacuum into which the Davidic Prince must emerge.

## 13. Summary of Chapter Two
- Moses foretold exile and regathering.
- Both houses of Israel were scattered—Ephraim first, Judah later.
- The Davidic monarchy collapsed, but the covenant did not.
- Hosea, Jeremiah, and Ezekiel promise a future Davidic ruler.
- This ruler appears **after** the exile, in the **latter days.**
- Restoration requires a Davidic shepherd-prince to reunite the tribes.
- The DSS confirm ancient Israelite belief in a future Davidic ruler during the restoration.
- The exile set the stage for the final and eternal fulfillment of the Davidic Covenant.

The Davidic Prince cannot be understood apart from the exile.

His mission is the reversal of exile and the restoration of the covenant people.

CHAPTER THREE

# THE RISE OF THE DAVIDIC PRINCE: PROPHECY OF A FUTURE LEADER

The collapse of the monarchy during the exile seemed to signal the death of the Davidic dynasty. The throne was empty, the Temple destroyed, and the people scattered across foreign lands. Yet in the midst of this collapse, the prophets began to speak with astonishing clarity about a future ruler—a **Davidic Prince** who would arise in the latter days to shepherd, unite, and govern all twelve tribes of Yashar'el.

This figure is described in:

- Hosea 3
- Jeremiah 30
- Ezekiel 34
- Ezekiel 37
- Psalms
- Isaiah
- The Dead Sea Scrolls
- The Pseudepigrapha
- Ancient Israelite restoration texts

This chapter explores:

1. The prophetic profile of the Davidic Prince
2. His titles in Scripture and their meanings
3. His distinction from the divine Messiah
4. His end-time appearance during Israel's restoration
5. His characteristics as a ruler
6. His relationship to the covenant
7. His portrayal in the Dead Sea Scrolls
8. His role in shepherding the reunited tribes
9. The theological necessity of his rise
10. How ancient Israelites expected him to function
11. Clues about his character, personality, and calling

This chapter is foundational. Where Chapter One established the covenant, and Chapter Two established the exile and prophetic necessity for restoration, **Chapter Three establishes the identity and role of the Princ himself.**

## 1. The Prophets Speak of a Future Davidic Leader

The prophets consistently refer to a Davidic figure who will arise **after the exile,** in the **latter days,** to lead the restored nation.

The most explicit examples:
**Hosea 3:5 (KJV)**
*"Afterward shall the children of Israel return, and seek Yahuah their Elohim, and David their king... in the latter days."*

Key observations:
- "Afterward" = after exile
- "Children of Israel" = Northern + Southern tribes
- "Return" = physical regathering
- "Seek David their king" = a Davidic ruler
- "Latter days" = eschatological timeframe

Hosea prophesied:
- A revival
- A return
- A national repentance
- A Davidic ruler over the restored tribes

No Israelite prophet ever contradicts this.

## 2. Jeremiah Confirms David's Future Role

Jeremiah speaks of the time immediately following Jacob's Trouble (the Great Tribulation).

**Jeremiah 30:9 (KJV)**
*They shall serve Yahuah their Elohim, and David their king, whom I will raise up unto them.*

Key words:
- "Raise up" = resurrection language, OR restore the line
- "Unto them" = to the people in the last days
- Happens after Jacob's Trouble

Jeremiah's prophecy:
- Shows David's restored throne
- Places it after the tribulation
- Confirms a literal ruler

## 3. Ezekiel Describes the Prince with Precision

Ezekiel is the most detailed.

**Ezekiel 34:23–24 (KJV)**
*23 And I will set up one shepherd over them... even my servant David.*
*24 ...and my servant David a prince among them.*

Here David is:
- A shepherd
- A leader
- A prince (not King of Kings)
-  Among the people
- Appointed by Yahuah

Ezekiel 37 repeats the prophecy with even greater clarity.

**Ezekiel 37:24–25 (KJV)**
*24 And David my servant shall be king over them…*
*25 …and my servant David shall be their prince for ever.*

These passages describe:
- A mortal ruler
- Over a united Israel
- Under Yahuah's eternal presence
- In the Millennial Kingdom

This cannot be Mashiach Yahusha because:
- The Prince offers sin offerings (Ezek. 45:22)
- The Prince has sons (Ezek. 46:16)
- The Prince receives tribal land allotments (Ezek. 48:21–22)
- The Prince submits to the Zadokite priesthood (Ezek. 44:9–16)
- The Prince is "among them" (Ezek. 34:24), not above humanity

This is a **human ruler,** not the divine Messiah.

## 4. Titles of the Davidic Prince and Their Meaning
The prophetic titles reveal his character and role.

### 1. "David" (Beloved)
A title of royal lineage.

### 2. "My servant David"
A term used for:
- Moses
- Isaiah
- The Messiah
- The faithful of Yahuah

It denotes obedience and calling.

### 3. "One shepherd"
He unites:
- Judah
- Ephraim
- All twelve tribes

### 4. "Prince" (Hebrew: נָשִׂיא — Nasi)
Not "King of Kings."
The term means:
- Leader
- Representative
- Appointed governor
- Ruler under a higher authority

### 5. "Branch of David" (in DSS and prophetic writings)
Symbol of new life springing from the Davidic stump.

### 6. "Messiah of Israel" (DSS terminology)
A Davidic anointed ruler—distinct from the Priest-Messiah.
These titles together portray:
- A revived Davidic lineage
- A shepherd-warrior
- A righteous governor
- A man under divine and priestly authority
- A restorer of the tribes

### 5. The Prince Is Distinct From the Divine Messiah
Prophets describe **two different figures** with different characteristics.
**Mashiach Yahusha is:**
- Divine
- Eternal
- Sinless
- Superior to all priests
- Not associated with land inheritance
- Not required to make sin offerings
- The universal King of Kings

The Davidic Prince is:
- Human
- Mortal
- Has sons

- Dependent upon priestly mediation
- Assigned specific land
- Must offer sin offerings
- Called "prince" not "king" in Ezekiel 40–48

Why two figures?

Because the Davidic Covenant and Ezekiel's Temple require:

1. A divine King
2. A human administrative ruler

The divine Messiah reigns over heaven and earth; the Davidic Prince reigns over **restored Yashar'el.**

## 6. The Prince Appears After the Regathering

The Prince's role is tied to:

- The return of the people
- The reunification of the tribes
- The establishment of the Millennial Temple

Ezekiel 40–48 shows:

- A physical prince
- Walking in the Temple
- Eating bread before Yahuah
- Administrating gates and offerings
- Governing the land allotments

Thus, the Prince appears only **after:**

- Israel returns
- The kingdom is restored
- The Temple is rebuilt
- The glory of Yahuah returns

His appearance is tied to Yahuah's tangible presence returning to Zion.

## 7. The Character of the Davidic Prince

Prophetic texts reveal much about his personality:

### A. He is humble

He is a "shepherd," not a tyrant.

### B. He is obedient

Called "My servant," which is a title of complete submission.

### C. He is righteous

Ezekiel contrasts him against wicked princes of the past.

## D. He is compassionate
Shepherds tend, gather, heal, and protect.

## E. He is courageous
He leads in warfare (as confirmed by DSS).

## F. He is wise and just
He judges fairly, unlike corrupt rulers of the past.

## G. He is anointed by Yahuah
He is appointed, not self-elevated.

## H. He is a unifier
He brings together Judah and Ephraim.

## I. He is faithful to Torah
He operates within the covenant system restored in Ezekiel's Temple.

## J. He is a restorer
He returns the land to the twelve tribes in their correct order.

The Davidic Prince is thus a righteous, Spirit-guided ruler whose leadership reflects the heart of Yahuah.

## 8. The Davidic Prince in the Dead Sea Scrolls
The DSS provide some of the clearest extra-biblical descriptions of thE Prince. DSS Titles for Him:
- Prince of the Congregation (נשיא העדה)
- Messiah of Israel
- Branch of David
- Leader of the Tribal Chiefs
- End-time Warrior

Key Passages:
**1QM 5:1–2**

    Prince of the Congregation leads the men of war.

**1QM 7:5–6**

    Priest leads spiritually; Prince leads militarily.

**1QM 17:5–9**
Yahuah appoints the Prince over the tribal leaders.

**4Q285 (Messianic Apocalypse)**
Branch of David and Prince of the Congregation destroy the enemies.

**4Q174 (Florilegium)**
Branch of David arises in the last days.

**1QS IX, 11**
Expectation of two Messiahs:
Priest-Messiah and Messiah of Israel (Davidic).

**DSS Conclusions:**
- The Prince is **Davidic**
- He is **future**
- He is a **warrior-deliverer**
- He works with a **Priestly Messiah**
- He rises in the **last days**
- He leads **all twelve tribes**
- He governs the restored nation
- He is a mortal anointed ruler under Yahuah

This is identical to Ezekiel's portrayal.

## 9. The Prince as Shepherd of Reunited Israel
Ezekiel 37 describes:
- Dry bones coming to life
- Judah and Ephraim being reunited
- One king over them
- One shepherd
- One covenant
- One land
- One nation

The Prince's role is pastoral:
- He gathers the lost
- He feeds the flock
- He heals the wounds
- He protects the vulnerable
- He enforces justice
- He shepherds with righteousness

His leadership style mirrors David's early years:

- Humble beginnings
- Zeal for Yahuah
- Courage against giants
- Loyalty to covenant
- Protection of the people
- Mercy toward enemies

He leads not through oppression, but through righteousness.


## 10. Why the Rise of the Prince Is Theologically Necessary

Without the Prince:

- The Davidic Covenant would fail
- Ezekiel's Temple would lack a ruler
- Tribal allotments could not be assigned
- The Shepherd prophecies could not be fulfilled
- The reunification of the tribes would lack leadership
- The covenant of peace could not be administered
- Israel would lack a representative for offerings
- The restoration would lack governmental structure

The Prince completes:

- The covenant
- The kingdom
- The restoration
- The Temple
- The priesthood
- The tribal system
- The national identity of Yashar'el

His presence is the capstone of Israelite eschatology.


## 11. Clues About the Prince's End-Time Identity

A composite picture emerges:

**A. He is a descendant of David**

Literal, not symbolic.

**B. He may come from obscurity**

As David did from shepherding fields.

**C. He appears in the latter days**

After Israel awakens.

**D. He rises during national distress**

Jacob's Trouble.

**E. He is chosen and anointed directly by Yahuah**

Not by political systems.

**F. He is intimately familiar with suffering**

A shepherd shaped by hardship.

**G. He is courageous and battle-proven**

As per DSS descriptions.

**H. He is morally upright**

In contrast to corrupt rulers of the past.

**I. He is deeply faithful to Yahuah**

Like David before him.

**J. He is protector and defender of the remnant**

A champion of the scattered tribes.

This portrait is of a humble, righteous, Spirit-led, covenant-honoring Israelite ruler restored in the last days.

## 12. Summary of Chapter Three

- The prophets unanimously predict a future Davidic ruler.
- This ruler is not Mashiach Yahusha but a human prince.
- He appears after exile, during the restoration of Israel.
- His titles reflect humility, strength, and divine appointment.
- Ezekiel describes his duties inside the Millennial Temple.
- The Dead Sea Scrolls identify him as the Prince of the Congregation.
- He leads Israel militarily and administratively.
- He unites the twelve tribes under one shepherd.
- His character reflects righteousness, humility, and courage.
- He is essential for the fulfillment of the Davidic Covenant.

The rise of the Davidic Prince is not merely a prophetic curiosity; it is the heart of Israel's restoration and the divine plan for the latter days.

---

CHAPTER FOUR

# THE SHEPHERD-KING: THE CHARACTER, HEART, AND ROLE OF THE END-TIME DAVIDIC PRINCE

The prophetic image of the Davidic Prince is not merely political or administrative. Scripture presents him as a shepherd, a servant, a leader, and a prince whose heart embodies the qualities that defined David, the son of Jesse. The prophets consistently paint this latter-day ruler as a man molded by Yahuah Himself—shaped through hardship, humbled by adversity, and elevated by divine appointment.

This chapter explores:
- The biblical meaning of a shepherd-king
- David's heart as the prophetic model
- The character traits of the end-time Prince
- His responsibilities toward the flock of Yashar'el
- His relationship to Yahuah, the Torah, and the priesthood
- His role in unifying the twelve tribes
- His function as ruler in the Millennial Kingdom
- How the Dead Sea Scrolls portray his character
- The spiritual qualities that distinguish him
- Signs that reveal his identity and calling

This chapter dives deeply into the **inner qualities** that make the Davidic Prince the ideal shepherd for Yahuah's restored nation.

## 1. The Biblical Image of the Shepherd King

In Scripture, the term **shepherd** represents:
- Leadership
- Protection
- Tenderness
- Guidance
- Provision
- Courage
- Sacrifice

Before David ruled as king, he ruled as a shepherd in the fields of Bethlehem. This was no accident. The shepherd is the symbol of the ideal king in the Tanakh.

**Psalm 78:70–72 (KJV)**
*70 He chose David also his servant, and took him from the sheepfolds:*
*71 From following the ewes great with young he brought him to feed Jacob his people, and Israel his inheritance.*
*72 So he fed them according to the integrity of his heart; and guided them by the skilfulness of his hands.*

This verse reveals three critical elements of true leadership:

    1.**Integrity of heart** — Character

    2.**Skillfulness of hands** — Competence

    3.**Shepherding posture** — Care and humility

The end-time Davidic Prince inherits this shepherd identity.

## 2. David as the Pattern for the Latter Day Prince

Every prophetic description of the end-time Prince uses **David** as the model —not Solomon, not Hezekiah, not Josiah, but David.

**Why David?**

Because:

- David loved Yahuah with his whole heart
- David defended Yashar'el from enemies
- David unified the tribes
- David honored the covenant
- David walked in humility
- David refused to exalt himself
- David confessed and repented when he sinned
- David never worshiped foreign gods

The end-time Prince carries this same spirit and calling.

**Key attributes of David that reappear in the Prince:**

**1. Courageous faith**

David faced Goliath alone; the Prince faces the nations.

**2. Zeal for Yahuah**

David said, "The zeal of Your house has eaten me up."

**3. Righteous judgment**

David judged the people with fairness; the Prince restores justice.

**4. Devotion to Torah**

David meditated on the Torah day and night.

**5. Deep humility**

David said, "Who am I, O Yahuah?" despite being king.

These attributes collectively define the character of the Davidic Prince.

## 3. The Character of the End-Time Prince According to Ezekiel

Ezekiel gives the fullest portrait of his character.

**A. He is obedient**

He follows Yahuah's statutes (Ezek. 37:24).

**B. He is humble**

Called "a prince among them," not above them (Ezek. 34:24).

**C. He is righteous**
He corrects the injustices of past leaders (Ezek. 45:9).
**D. He is pure-hearted**
He does not oppress the people or seize land unfairly (Ezek. 46:18).
**E. He is honorable**
He honors the Temple ordinances and the priesthood (Ezek. 44–46).
**F. He is steadfast**
He leads the nation generation after generation (Ezek. 37:25).
**G. He is courageous**
He governs during the fallout of the end-time war.
**H. He is loyal to Yahuah**
He offers sacrifices in humility before Yahuah's presence (Ezek. 45:22).
**I. He is just**
He ensures fair inheritance laws (Ezek. 46:17–18).
**J. He is compassionate**
He shepherds the flock with tender care (Ezek. 34:23).
This combination of traits forms a ruler who is uniquely suited to restore Yashar'el.

## 4. The Prince's Relationship to Yahuah: Servant, Not Sovereign
The Prince is described repeatedly as **"My servant David"** (Ezek. 34:23; 37:24).
This title means:
- He is not divine
- He is not worshiped
- He is a servant leader
- He is under Yahuah's authority
- His success depends on obedience
- His calling is covenantal

This servant identity mirrors:
- Moses
- Joshua
- Isaiah
- David

The Prince's entire identity is framed by submission to Yahuah.

## 5. His Relationship to Torah: Guardian of Righteousness
Ezekiel stresses that the Prince will:
- Walk in Yahuah's ordinances
- Keep His statutes

65

- Enforce Torah justice
- Restore righteous judgment

**Ezekiel 37:24**
*...and they shall also walk in my judgments, and observe my statutes, and do them.*
The Prince does not invent new laws. He restores the original covenantal laws. He becomes a guardian of righteousness in Yashar'el.

### 6. His Relationship to the Priests: Submission and Partnership
The books of Ezekiel and the DSS both reveal a dual leadership system:
1. Priests — spiritual authority
2. Prince — civil authority

The Prince submits to the sons of Zadok, who:
1. Teach Torah
2. Offer sacrifices
3. Maintain purity
4. Govern worship

The Prince's role is complementary, not superior.

### Ezekiel 44–48 establishes a partnership:
- Priests handle the holy things
- The Prince oversees the people
- Both guard righteousness in the land

This model avoids the corruption that ruined Israel's kings in the past.

### 7. His Role in Reuniting the Twelve Tribes
One of the Prince's greatest responsibilities is the reunification of:
- **Judah** (Southern Kingdom)
- **Ephraim / Israel** (Northern Tribes)

This reunification is one of the most powerful prophecies in all Scripture.

### Ezekiel 37:22
*I will make them one nation... and one king shall be king to them all.*
*The Prince is the human instrument that carries this out.*

Responsibilities in reunification:
1. Healing historic divisions
2. Restoring tribal identity
3. Reestablishing tribal allotments

4. Instituting covenant unity

5. Leading the nation as one flock under one shepherd

The Prince brings shalom (restoration) where there was once division.

## 8. The Prince's Role in the Millennial Kingdom

His responsibilities include:

### A. Governing the Land

He receives territory between Judah and Benjamin (Ezek. 48:21–22).

### B. Maintaining Justice

He ensures fairness in land distribution (Ezek. 45:8).

### C. Overseeing Temple Worship

He enters through the eastern gate on Sabbaths and New Moons (Ezek. 46:1–2).

### D. Offering Sacrifices

He presents offerings on behalf of himself and the people (Ezek. 45:17, 22).

### E. Feasting with the People

He participates in communal meals in the courts of the Temple (Ezek. 46:10).

### F. Leading National Worship

He leads the nation before Yahuah in appointed times.

### G. Representing the People

He stands as the earthly representative of Yashar'el before Yahuah.

### H. Enforcing Covenant Law

He ensures Torah is followed throughout the land.

### I. Guiding the People into Righteousness

He becomes the visible example of obedience.

### J. Maintaining Peace

He guards against injustice and oppression.

This is not symbolic—it is literal administration under Yahuah's Kingdom rule.

## 9. The Portrait of the Prince in the Dead Sea Scrolls

The DSS describe him as:

### 1. Humble

A servant leader, not a tyrant.

### 2. Righteous

Called the "Messiah of Israel" because of his anointing.

### 3. Courageous

He leads the Sons of Light against the Sons of Darkness (1QM).

**4. Wise**
He judges with understanding and fairness.
**5. Appointed by Yahuah**
1QM 17 says Yahuah "empowers and appoints him."
**6. Guardian of the Tribes**
He is set over the leaders of the tribes (1QM 17:5–9).
**7. A Branch of David**
4Q285 and 4Q174 identify him as the Davidic Branch.
**8. A restorer of justice**
He removes wickedness from the midst of the people.
**9. A man of war**
He participates in Yahuah's final deliverance.
**10. A partner to the Priestly Messiah**
1QS IX, 11 describes "Messiahs of Aaron and Israel."
Thus the DSS emphasize:

- Righteousness
- Humility
- War leadership
- Tribal governance
- Priestly cooperation

All matching Ezekiel's vision.

## 10. The Spiritual Qualities That Distinguish the Prince
The Prince's leadership is defined by internal qualities:
**A. Fear of Yahuah**
He leads in reverence, not arrogance.
**B. Discernment**
He understands the times and the needs of the people.
**C. Compassion**
He binds up the broken and brings back the scattered.
**D. Integrity**
He operates with complete transparency and fairness.
**E. Faithfulness**
He walks consistently in obedience.
**F. Courage**
He faces opposition boldly, like David before Goliath.
**G. Purity of Heart**
He does not pursue idolatry, greed, or power.
**H. Selflessness**
He lays down his life for the flock.

**I. Patience**
He shepherds people who are recovering from trauma and dispersion.
**J. Zeal for Yahuah**
He defends the holiness of Yahuah's Name.
These qualities make him the perfect covenant leader.

## 11. Clues About the Prince's Life and Calling
While Scripture does not name the Prince, it gives hints about his life:
**1. He rises unexpectedly**
Like David, who was overlooked.
**2. He experiences suffering**
Shaped through hardship.
**3. He is from the remnant**
Not a foreign ruler.
**4. He is anointed by Yahuah alone**
Not by earthly politics.
**5. He is hidden until the appointed time**
Revealed only when Yahuah lifts him up.
**6. He is deeply connected to Yashar'el's awakening**
He rises alongside national repentance.
**7. He comes after tribulation**
Jeremiah 30:9 places his appearance after Jacob's Trouble.
**8. He is recognized by the righteous**
Those who know Torah see his calling.
**9. He is empowered by the Spirit**
Like David in 1 Samuel 16:13.
**10. He leads under Yahuah's direct authority**
He carries a divine mandate.

## 12. Summary of Chapter Four
- The Davidic Prince is a shepherd-king after Yahuah's heart.
- His character mirrors David—humble, courageous, righteous.
- He is the ideal servant leader for restored Yashar'el.
- He works in submission to the priesthood and the Torah.
- He unites the twelve tribes of Yashar'el.
- His role is central in the Millennial Kingdom.
- The Dead Sea Scrolls confirm his humility, courage, and divine appointment.
- His leadership style is compassionate, just, and Spirit-anointed.
- He rises in the last days as part of the great restoration.

- He fulfills the covenantal and pastoral role David foreshadowed.

The Prince's character is the heart of his calling. His righteousness prepares the way for the covenant of peace and the full restoration of Yashar'el.

CHAPTER FIVE

# THE DAVIDIC PRINCE IN THE LATTER DAYS: SIGNS, TIMING, AND THE RETURN OF YASHAR'EL

The rise of the Davidic Prince is inseparable from the prophetic sequence of the last days. The Scriptures paint a comprehensive picture of when this ruler appears, what conditions surround his coming, how Yashar'el recognizes him, and what signs accompany his appointment. His emergence is the culmination of centuries of covenant expectation, the reversal of the exile, and the restoration of the Kingdom of Yahuah on earth.

This chapter explores:
- The prophetic timeline of the latter days
- The crisis that precedes the Prince's rise
- The regathering of the twelve tribes
- The spiritual awakening of Yashar'el
- The national repentance that prepares the Prince's coming
- The role of Jacob's Trouble
- The Prince's appearance during and after the Great Tribulation
- Signs that reveal his identity
- The Dead Sea Scrolls' view of end-time timing
- The Prince as a sign of restoration
- The Messiah-Prince relationship in the last days
- The Prince's role in the dawn of the Millennial Kingdom

This chapter offers a prophetic map for understanding when and how the Davidic Prince emerges in the last days.

## 1. The Prophetic Timeline of the Last Days
The prophets give a clear order of events surrounding the restoration of Yashar'el.
- The sequence is:
- Scattering of all twelve tribes
- Long absence of king or prince (Hosea 3:4)
- Awakening of the remnant
- Seeking Yahuah and His ways
- National repentance and return
- Jacob's Trouble (Jer. 30:7)
- Deliverance by Yahuah
- Regathering of the tribes (Ezek. 37:21)
- Reunification of Judah and Ephraim (Ezek. 37:15–22)
- Installation of the Davidic Prince (Ezek. 37:24–25)
- Millennial Temple established (Ezek. 40–48)
- Covenant of Peace and eternal presence of Yahuah (Ezek. 37:26–28)

The Prince emerges after:
- The exile
- The scattering
- The awakening
- The tribulation
- The national repentance
- he uniting of the two sticks

He appears before:
- The Millennial Temple administration
- The tribal allotments
- The eternal presence of Yahuah dwelling in the land

The Prince is thus placed between Jacob's Trouble and the Millennial Kingdom.

## 2. The Crisis That Precedes the Prince: A World in Upheaval

Scripture repeatedly ties the Prince's rise to a global crisis.

**Jeremiah 30:7 (KJV)**

*Alas! for that day is great, so that none is like it: it is even the time of Jacob's trouble…*

This is:
- A time of oppression
- War
- Confusion
- Persecution
- Distress among the nations
- Fear and trembling
- Judgment on the wicked

It is in this context that the Prince appears.

**Jeremiah 30:9**

*But they shall serve Yahuah their Elohim, and David their king…*

Thus:
- Crisis precedes restoration
- Distress precedes enthronement
- Tribulation precedes the rising of David

The Prince does not emerge during national peace, but during national shaking.

### 3. The Regathering of the Twelve Tribes
The Prince does not come until Yashar'el begins to awaken to her identity.
**Ezekiel 37:21–22**
*Behold, I will take the children of Israel from among the nations… and gather them… and I will make them one nation… and one king shall be king to them all.*

Three key facts:
**1. The gathering is global**
"From among the nations" refers to every continent.
**2. It includes all twelve tribes**
Not only Judah.
**3. It precedes the Prince's installation**
The Prince rules over the **united** nation.
This means the Prince appears **after** the awakening of the scattered remnant.

### 4. The Spiritual Awakening of Yashar'el
Another sign of the Prince's arrival is the spiritual renewal of the people.
**Hosea 3:5**
*Afterward shall the children of Israel return, and seek Yahuah their Elohim…*

This "seeking" includes:
- Returning to Torah
- Restored covenant identity
- Rejecting idols
- Restoring the Name of Yahuah
- Uncovering true Israelite heritage
- Repenting for the sins of the forefathers
- A yearning for righteousness
- Longing for the Shepherd-King

This awakening is not geographic—it is spiritual. It is the internal preparation of Yashar'el for the Prince.

### 5. National Repentance as a Prerequisite
Prophets show that repentance is necessary for restoration.
**Deuteronomy 30:1–3**
Yashar'el's return occurs when they "call to mind" the Torah and repent.
**Ezekiel 36:24–28**

Yahuah cleanses, restores, and gives a new heart.
**Zechariah 12:10–14**
The house of David and the inhabitants of Jerusalem weep in repentance.
**Hosea 5:15–6:2**
Israel acknowledges its sin and seeks Yahuah.
This repentance prepares the way for:

- Restoration
- Reunification
- Covenant renewal
- The rise of the Prince

Repentance is the womb in which the Prince is revealed.

## 6. Jacob's Trouble and the Prince's Emergence
The Prince rises **during or immediately after** the greatest tribulation Israel has ever faced.
**Why?**
Because Scripture places the reappearance of David **after** Jacob's Trouble (Jer. 30:9).
Jacob's Trouble is:

- The dark night before dawn
- The final refining of the remnant
- The breaking of the nations
- The shaking of Babylon
- The collapse of false systems
- The humbling of Yashar'el
- The cleansing before restoration

The Prince emerges after the nation is humbled, ready to be shepherded.
His leadership is the answer to national trauma.

## 7. The Prince's Appearance in the Prophetic Sequence
Prophet after prophet repeats the same order:

- **Scattering**
- **Awakening**
- **Tribulation**
- **Deliverance by Yahuah**
- **Return to the land**
- **Reunification**
- **Appointment of the Prince**
- **Millennial Kingdom established**

The Prince appears between Stage 5 and Stage 8:

- When Yashar'el is restored
- When the tribes are reunited
- When the covenant is renewed
- When the Temple is rebuilt

He becomes the first human ruler of the restored Kingdom.

## 8. Signs That Reveal the Identity of the Prince

Scripture gives numerous signs for recognizing the Davidic Prince.

**1. Lineage from David**

A descendant of the royal line.

**2. Hidden before elevation**

Like David in the fields.

**3. Raised up by Yahuah, not man**

Jeremiah 30:9 — Yahuah raises him.

**4. Appears among the remnant**

Ezekiel says he is "among them" (Ezek. 34:24).

**5. Recognized through righteousness**

He exemplifies Torah obedience.

**6. A shepherd's heart**

Compassion for the scattered flock.

**7. Courage during crisis**

Rises in days of distress, not peace.

**8. Spirit of wisdom and judgment**

He restores justice in the land.

**9. Submitted to the priesthood**

He cooperates with the sons of Zadok.

**10. Restorer of the tribes**

He enforces the new land allotments.

**11. A builder of unity**

He ends the division between Judah and Ephraim.

**12. A restorer of righteousness**

He does not oppress the people.

**13. Empowered supernaturally**

Like David, the Spirit of Yahuah rests upon him.

These signs collectively paint the picture of a leader molded by Yahuah.

## 9. The Dead Sea Scrolls Confirm Timing and Signs

The DSS depict the Prince emerging:

- During the eschatological war

- After the corruption of priesthood and monarchy
- Among a remnant who seeks purity
- In partnership with a Priestly Messiah
- As a Davidic war-leader
- When Israel is being restored
- As a figure appointed directly by Yahuah

The War Scroll (1QM) explicitly describes him rising in the last days to lead:

- The tribes
- The righteous remnant
- The Sons of Light
- The people in battle against oppression

This aligns with:

- Jeremiah
- Ezekiel
- Hosea
- Isaiah
- Zechariah

The DSS confirm that ancient Israelites believed the Prince's appearance was tied to the final events of history.

## 10. The Prince as the Sign of National Restoration

His appearance is not only a result of restoration—it is a **sign of it.**
The Prince signals:

- Yahuah has returned to the covenant
- The tribes are awakening
- The captivity is ending
- The covenant is being renewed
- Justice is being restored
- The Kingdom is being rebuilt
- The Millennial Temple is imminent

He is the living sign of Ezekiel 37 fulfilled.
His rule announces:
**"The kingdom has returned to Yashar'el."**

## 11. The Prince and the Messiah in the Latter Days

The Davidic Prince is **not the divine Messiah,** yet he works under the Messiah's authority. Their relationship is complementary:
**The Messiah**

- Reigns eternally

- Judges universally
- Is divine, eternal, perfect
- Subdues the nations
- Rebuilds Yahuah's dwelling among men

**The Davidic Prince**
- Reigns on earth over Yashar'el
- Governs the twelve tribes
- Is mortal and covenant-bound
- Restores justice at the tribal level
- Oversees Temple and land administration

The Prince is the earthly steward of the divine King.
This dual leadership is seen in:
- Ezekiel's prophetic structure
- The dual-Messiah model of the DSS
- Isaiah's distinction between divine rule and earthly governance
- The Torah's pattern of priest and king

The Prince is the instrument through which the Messiah's rule is carried out on earth.

## 12. The Dawn of the Millennial Kingdom and the Prince's Installation

The Prince's installation is the beginning of a new age:
- Yahuah restores His presence
- The Temple is rebuilt
- The land is redistributed
- The covenant of peace is established
- Death is restrained
- Justice flows from Zion
- Yahuah dwells among His people forever

The Prince is the first human ruler of this restored kingdom. His leadership marks the dawn of a new era.

## 13. Summary of Chapter Five
- The Prince appears during the restoration of Yashar'el in the last days.
- His emergence follows Jacob's Trouble but precedes the Millennial Kingdom.
- National repentance, awakening, and regathering prepare the way for him.
- He is revealed through righteousness, humility, and divine appointment.

- The Dead Sea Scrolls confirm his role as the end-time leader of Israel.
- He is a sign of the covenant's final fulfillment.
- He stands under the authority of the divine Messiah yet governs
- Yashar'el.
- His installation marks the beginning of the Millennial Kingdom.

The rise of the Davidic Prince is the climax of prophetic history and the fulfillment of Yahuah's covenant promises.

CHAPTER SIX

# THE PRINCE AND THE COVENANT OF PEACE: RESTORING ORDER, JUSTICE, AND HOLINESS IN THE KINGDOM OF YAHUAH

The rise of the Davidic Prince is inseparable from the establishment of the **Covenant of Peace**—a prophetic promise in Scripture that signals the dawn of a restored, righteous, and unified Yashar'el. This covenant is not merely spiritual; it is tangible, legal, national, and generational. It includes land, leadership, worship, justice, and the direct dwelling of Yahuah among His people.

In this chapter, we examine:
1. What the Covenant of Peace is
2. Its origins in the Torah
3. Its prophetic development in Isaiah, Jeremiah, and Ezekiel
4. Its connection to the Davidic Prince
5. How the Prince administers this covenant
6. The restoration of divine order in the land
7. The reestablishment of justice
8. The purification of worship
9. The return of Yahuah's presence
10. The Prince's role in maintaining holiness and unity
11. How the Dead Sea Scrolls anticipated this covenant
12. The long-term effects of the covenant on the Millennial Kingdom

This chapter shows how the Prince becomes the chief earthly steward of Yahuah's renewed covenantal order.

## 1. What Is the Covenant of Peace?
The term appears explicitly in Ezekiel 34 and Ezekiel 37:

**Ezekiel 34:25 (KJV)**
*And I will make with them a covenant of peace, and will cause the evil beasts to cease out of the land...*

**Ezekiel 37:26 (KJV)**
*Moreover I will make a covenant of peace with them; it shall be an everlasting covenant with them...*

The Covenant of Peace includes:
- National restoration
- Removal of oppression
- Unity of the tribes
- Holiness in worship

- Justice in the land
- Security from enemies
- Everlasting presence of Yahuah
- A righteous leader (the Prince)
- A purified priesthood (sons of Zadok)

This covenant forms the constitutional foundation of the restored Kingdom.

## 2. The Roots of the Covenant of Peace in the Torah

The concept is rooted in multiple Torah passages:

### A. Numbers 25:12–13 — The Priestly Covenant of Peace

Given to **Phinehas**, establishing a covenant of:
- Peace
- Priesthood
- Righteousness

This sets a precedent:

**The Covenant of Peace requires righteous leadership.**

### B. Leviticus 26:3–13 — Blessings for obedience

Describes a Torah-based peace:
- No fear of enemies
- Fruitfulness
- Yahuah dwelling among Israel
- Covenant faithfulness

### C. Deuteronomy 30 — Restoration after repentance

A covenant renewal after exile.

### D. Isaiah 54:10 — Everlasting Covenant of Peace

Ties peace to Yahuah's unfailing love.

Thus, the Covenant of Peace is:
- Restorative
- Obedience-based
- Righteousness-centered
- And connected to leadership

In the latter days, all these elements converge in the Prince.

## 3. Ezekiel's Revelation: The Covenant of Peace + Davidic Prince

Ezekiel is the clearest:

**Ezekiel 37:24–26 (KJV)**
*24 And David my servant shall be king over them…*
*25 …my servant David shall be their prince for ever.*
*26 Moreover I will make a covenant of peace with them…*
Here is the structure:
>    1.Davidic Prince installed
>    2.Everlasting covenant established
>    3.Sanctuary placed among Israel
>    4.Yahuah's presence dwelling forever

The Prince is thus the human overseer of the covenant.

## 4. What Does the Covenant of Peace Accomplish?
### A. Ends internal oppression
Ezekiel 45:9—No more violence or unjust gain.
### B. Establishes just governance
The Prince ensures fairness and righteousness.
### C. Ensures land integrity
The Prince prevents oppression through land seizure (Ezek. 46:18).
### D. Restores righteous worship
The Temple system of Ezekiel 40–48 is purified and sanctified.
### E. Reunites the tribes
Ezekiel 37 brings the two sticks into one.
### F. Secures Israel from enemies
Ezekiel 34:25—No evil beasts, no threats.
### G. Reestablishes Torah obedience
Ezekiel 37:24—The Prince causes the people to walk in Yahuah's laws.
### H. Connects heaven and earth
Yahuah's glory returns to Zion (Ezek. 43:1–7).
Thus, the covenant is comprehensive.

## 5. The Prince's Role in Administering the Covenant
The Prince is not just a symbolic figure—he is the earthly administrator of the kingdom's legal structure.
His primary roles include:
### 1. Enforcing justice
Ezekiel 45:8–9 commands him to keep the land free from oppression.
### 2. Preventing tyranny
He may not seize inheritance from the people (Ezek. 46:18).
### 3. Overseeing offerings
He provides offerings for festivals and Sabbaths (Ezek. 45:17).

## 4. Leading national worship
Ezekiel 46:1–12 places him at the forefront of Temple worship.
## 5. Maintaining order in the Temple
He can enter through specific gates; the people follow his lead.
## 6. Managing land allotments
He receives territory between Judah and Benjamin (Ezek. 48:21–22).
## 7. Governing all tribes
He oversees the distribution of tribal land (Ezek. 48:1–29).
## 8. Ensuring covenant faithfulness
He models obedience before the nation.
## 9. Defending the people
Ezekiel and DSS describe him as a protector.
## 10. Shepherding the flock
He provides pastoral leadership, not authoritarian rule.

Thus, the Prince is the constitutional monarch of restored Yashar'el—but under Yahuah's direct authority.

## 6. The Return of Holiness: The Sanctuary as the Heart of the Covenant

A major feature of the Covenant of Peace is the restoration of a holy sanctuary.

**Ezekiel 37:26–28**

*My sanctuary also shall be in the midst of them for evermore.*
*And the nations shall know that I Yahuah do sanctify Israel...*

The sanctuary serves as:

- The seat of divine presence
- The heart of worship
- The center of justice
- The guarantee of holiness
- The Prince's role is deeply tied to this sanctuary.

**He is not a priest, but he is the closest non-priest allowed to approach.**
This reflects ancient Israelite structure:

- Priests: spiritual sanctifiers
- Prince: civil sanctifier and covenant guardian

Together, they uphold holiness in the land.

## 7. Justice Restored: The Prince as Protector of the People

Past kings abused power. The Prince does not.

**Ezekiel 45:9**

*Enough, O princes of Israel: remove violence and spoil...*

The Prince:

- Ends corruption
- Ends unjust taxation
- Ends land theft
- Ends oppression
- Ends bribery
- Ends false judgment

He becomes the embodiment of righteous governance.

**This is the first time since David that Yashar'el experiences righteous rulership.**

## 8. Purifying the Worship System

Ezekiel 40–48 outlines a purified Temple system.

**The Prince's role:**

- Ensure purity
- Lead national worship
- Present offerings
- Maintain protocol
- Honor the priesthood
- Keep the appointed times

**Ezekiel 46:2–3**

*The prince shall enter by the way of the porch of that gate...*
*Likewise the people of the land shall worship...*

Here, the Prince:

- Models worship
- Leads by example
- Unites the people through ritual
- Ensures covenant fidelity

He is a worshiping ruler.

## 9. The Covenant of Peace in the Dead Sea Scrolls

The DSS do not use the exact phrase "Covenant of Peace," but they describe its components.

**Key DSS themes:**

**1. A righteous community**

Dedicated to purity and covenant order.

**2. A Davidic Prince**

Who leads the community and enforces justice.

### 3. A Priestly Messiah
Who purifies worship and teaches Torah.
### 4. A final war against oppression
Which leads to peace for Israel.
### 5. Yahuah's presence returning
To a purified Jerusalem.
### 6. Everlasting righteousness Flowing from the sanctuary.
In the DSS, the Prince of the Congregation is the one who:
- Defends the righteous
- Establishes justice
- Works with the priesthood
- Ushers in the final age of peace

This mirrors Ezekiel's Covenant of Peace perfectly.

## 10. The Prince as the Guardian of Holiness
The Prince guards:
- The land
- The people
- The borders
- The inheritance rights
- The sanctuary protocols
- The national righteousness
- The tribal unity

He becomes the earthly guardian of holiness, while the sons of Zadok are the spiritual guardians.

Together, they create a kingdom where:

**Holiness, justice, and peace are inseparable.**

## 11. Long-Term Effects of the Covenant of Peace
The Covenant of Peace produces:
### 1. Generational stability
"Everlasting covenant" (Ezek. 37:26).
### 2. Absence of fear
No oppression, no invasion.
### 3. Restored creation
The land yields abundantly again.
### 4. Spiritual renewal
A new heart and a new spirit.
### 5. National unity
Tribal division disappears.

**6. Righteous leadership**
No more corrupt rulers.
**7. True worship**
Purified Temple service.
**8. Universal witness**
The nations see Yahuah's power.
**9. Eternal presence**
Yahuah dwells among His people forever.
The Prince is central to this transformation.

## 12. Summary of Chapter Six
- The Covenant of Peace is the backbone of Israel's restoration.
- It is an everlasting covenant tied to the Davidic Prince.
- It restores justice, holiness, unity, and divine presence.
- The Prince is the chief earthly administrator of this covenant.
- He protects the people, enforces justice, and oversees worship.
- The sanctuary becomes the center of national life.
- The Prince and the priesthood work together to maintain holiness.
- The DSS confirm an end-time age of peace under a Davidic ruler.
- The Millennial Kingdom begins with the Prince's covenant steward-ship.

The Covenant of Peace is the fulfillment of ancient promises and the divine framework for the restored Kingdom of Yashar'el under the leadership of the Davidic Prince.

CHAPTER SEVEN

# THE PRINCE AND THE MILLENNIAL TEMPLE: HIS ROLE IN THE REBUILT HOUSE OF YAHUAH

The installation of the Davidic Prince coincides with the construction and consecration of the **Millennial Temple**—the colossal sanctuary described in Ezekiel chapters 40 through 48. This Temple, unlike the First and Second Temples, is not built by human initiative alone. It is revealed through divine vision, established in the era of restoration, and serves as the physical center of worship, justice, and national identity for all twelve tribes of Yashar'el.

This chapter explores:

1. The prophetic revelation of the Millennial Temple
2. Its significance in the Kingdom of Yahuah
3. The Prince's unique relationship to the Temple
4. His duties in worship and sacrifice
5. His role in the sanctification of the land
6. The Prince and the Eastern Gate
7. How the Temple reorders national life in Yashar'el
8. The meaning of Temple rituals in the restored kingdom
9. The relationship between the Prince and the sons of Zadok
10. The role of the Temple in uniting the tribes
11. The Dead Sea Scrolls' expectations of a restored sanctuary
12. The Prince as the first non-priestly man restored to holiness protocols
13. The Temple as the bridge between heaven and earth

This chapter reveals how the end-time Prince serves not merely as a political leader but as the **covenantal link between the people, the land, the priesthood, and the very presence of Yahuah.**

## 1. The Prophetic Vision of the Millennial Temple

Ezekiel receives the longest and most detailed description of a Temple anywhere in Scripture. The dimensions, gates, courts, chambers, altars, and ordinances occupy nine entire chapters (Ezek. 40–48).

Key features of the Temple:

- Enormous in size
- Perfectly symmetrical
- Designed to emphasize holiness
- Guarded by strict boundaries
- Administered by the sons of Zadok
- Governed jointly with the Davidic Prince

The Temple is not symbolic; it is literal, architectural, and spiritual.

**The Temple is the heart of the restored Kingdom.**

## 2. Why the Temple Must Be Rebuilt

The Temple is necessary because:

### 1. Yahuah returns to dwell among His people

Ezek. 43:1–7 describes the glory entering the east gate.

### 2. The covenant of peace centers on the sanctuary

Ezek. 37:26–28 emphasizes the sanctuary's centrality.

### 3. The Prince needs a place to administer worship

Ezek. 45–46 outline his actions within the Temple.

### 4. Israel must learn holiness again

The Temple's structure teaches separation between sacred and common.

### 5. The nations must recognize Yahuah's kingship

All nations come to worship (Isa. 2:2–4; Zech. 14:16–19).

### 6. The tribal order is restored

The Temple is placed at the center of the tribal allotments.

The Millennial Temple is thus the **spiritual, political, and geographical center** of the restored Kingdom.


## 3. The Prince as the Chief Lay Leader of the Temple

While the priests (sons of Zadok) administer the holy things, the Prince serves as the chief lay leader with unique access and responsibilities.

**He is the highest-ranking non-priest allowed into sacred zones.**

Ezekiel assigns him distinct duties:

- Offering sacrifices
- Leading worship
- Regulating feast observances
- Serving as the people's representative
- Entering specific gates
- Eating holy bread before Yahuah
- Ensuring justice in the land
- Maintaining Temple purity
- Overseeing the sanctuary's governance

This role is unprecedented in all Scripture.


## 4. The Prince's Entrance and Use of the Eastern Gate

One of the most sacred sections of Ezekiel's vision concerns the **Eastern Gate.**

**Ezekiel 44:1–3 (KJV)**

*1 Then he brought me back the way of the gate of the outward sanctuary which looketh toward the east; and it was shut.*

*2 Then said Yahuah unto me; This gate shall be shut, it shall not be*

*opened… because Yahuah, the Elohim of Israel, hath entered in by it…*
*3 It is for the Prince; the Prince, he shall sit in it to eat bread before Yahuah…*

**Key revelations:**
- The Eastern Gate is permanently shut
- No man may enter through it
- Because Yahuah's glory passed through it
- **Except the Prince**
- Who sits in this gate before Yahuah
- And eats the sacred covenant bread there

**This is the highest honor given to any mortal in Scripture.**

The Prince does not walk through the gate; he **enters by the porch** and sits within the threshold to worship.

This seat is a sign of:
- Favor
- Authority
- Covenant relationship
- Divine selection

It signifies the Prince's unique closeness to Yahuah.

## 5. The Prince's Liturgical Duties: Offerings and Worship

Ezekiel 45–46 describe the Prince's offerings:

**Ezekiel 45:17**

*It shall be the Prince's part to give burnt offerings, and meat offerings, and drink offerings, in the feasts, and in the new moons, and in the Sabbaths…*

**He provides offerings on behalf of:**
- Himself
- The people
- The nation
- The land

**His duties include:**
**A. Sin offering**
He offers for himself (Ezek. 45:22).

**B. Burnt and peace offerings**

During new moons and Sabbaths.

**C. Leading the people**

He enters and exits with them during worship (Ezek. 46:10).

**D. Presiding over feasts**

Such as Passover and Sukkot (Ezek. 45:21–25).

**E. Participating in communal meals**

Within the courts of the Temple.

The Prince thus serves as:

- Intercessor
- Worship leader
- Covenant representative
- National overseer
- Example of obedience

## 6. The Prince and the Priests: A Sacred Partnership

Ezekiel distinguishes sharply between:

- **The Priestly Order** — sons of Zadok
- **The Royal Order** — the Davidic Prince

**Responsibilities of the Sons of Zadok:**

- Offer sacrifices
- Teach and judge according to Torah
- Minister at the altar
- Enter the Holy Place
- Maintain sacred objects
- Govern ritual purity

**Responsibilities of the Prince:**

- Govern the people
- Protect inheritance rights
- Ensure justice
- Provide offerings
- Lead national worship
- Maintain civil order
- Oversee land allotments

Thus, the Prince and the Priests form a dual leadership:

- **Priests** = Spiritual sanctification
- **Prince** = Civil sanctification

This partnership reflects ancient Israel's original design:

- Moses (civil leader) + Aaron (high priest)
- Jehoshaphat (king) + Zadok (priest)

In the Millennial Kingdom, this divine order is restored perfectly.

## 7. The Temple's Design Reinforces the Prince's Role
Every architectural detail has spiritual significance.
### A. A separated holy district
The Temple is surrounded by a sanctified zone.
### B. The Prince's land grant
He receives land on both sides of the holy district (Ezek. 48:21–22).
### C. Gates for specific purposes
The Prince uses particular gates during feasts (Ezek. 46:2).
### D. Dining chambers for offerings
The Prince joins the priests in sacred meals (Ezek. 44:29).
### E. Special clothing requirements
The Prince's attire distinguishes him from priests but emphasizes purity.
### F. Boundary markers
No oppression, land theft, or corruption permitted.
The design teaches:
- Holiness
- Order
- ustice
- Division between sacred and common
- Respect for divine boundaries

The Prince is the first to model these principles.

## 8. The Temple as the Center of National Life
The Millennial Temple becomes more than a place of worship.
**It becomes:**
- The Supreme Court
- The National Assembly
- The educational center
- The cultural center
- The covenant headquarters
- The administrative heart of the nation

Under the Prince's leadership, the Temple transforms into the nucleus of Yahuah's kingdom on earth.

## 9. The Nation Reorganized Around the Sanctuary
The tribal allotments in Ezekiel 48 reveal a new national order:

**Seven tribes north of the sanctuary**

- Dan
- Asher
- Naphtali
- Manasseh
- Ephraim
- Reuben
- Judah

**Holy District & Prince's land**

In the center

**Five tribes south of the sanctuary**

- Benjamin
- Simeon
- Issachar
- Zebulun
- Gad

This arrangement ensures:

- Equal inheritance
- Justice in land
- Centering all tribes around the presence of Yahuah
- Constant access to worship
- National unity

The Prince enforces this allocation, preventing corruption.


## 10. The Purpose of Sacrifices in the Millennial Kingdom

Sacrifices in Ezekiel's Temple are not for:

- Providing salvation
- Replacing Messiah's atoning work

Instead, they serve:

### A. Memorial function

A physical reminder of sin and redemption.

### B. Covenant purification

The Temple must be cleansed regularly.

### C. Teaching function

Sacrifices re-teach holiness to the nations.

### D. Ritual participation

Believers enter a physical covenant rhythm.

### E. Governmental order

The Prince maintains national obedience.

### F. Symbolic restoration
Israel's ancient worship is restored in purified form.
The Prince ensures these sacrifices are administered according to Torah and Ezekiel's specific ordinances.

## 11. The Temple in the Dead Sea Scrolls
The DSS expected:
- A purified Temple
- A future sanctuary built in the last days
- A dual leadership system
- A Davidic Prince overseeing warfare and governance
- A Priestly Messiah overseeing worship
- A community living under strict holiness laws
- Yahuah's presence returning to a restored Zion

Texts such as:
- Temple Scroll (11QT)
- War Scroll (1QM)
- Rule of the Congregation (1QSa)
- Florilegium (4Q174)
- Mishmarot priestly courses

*...all anticipate a sanctified future Temple.*
This expectation aligns with Ezekiel 40–48 perfectly.

## 12. The Prince as the First Restored Man Allowed Near the Presence
Among all Israelites in the restored Kingdom:
- Only priests may approach the altar
- Only Zadokites may enter the Holy Place
- Only the Prince may sit in the Eastern Gate

The Prince is the closest non-priest to the divine presence.
The Eastern Gate seat symbolizes:
- Divine favor
- Covenant authority
- Restored relationship
- Acceptance by Yahuah

It elevates the Prince to a sacred governmental office unmatched by previous kings.

## 13. The Temple as the Bridge Between Heaven and Earth
The Temple symbolizes:
- Heaven's government on earth

- Divine justice replacing human corruption
- The presence of Yahuah dwelling among mortals
- The covenant order restored
- The nations streaming to Zion
- The unity of heaven and earth

The Prince stands at this intersection, representing Yashar'el before Yahuah and Yahuah's government before the people.

## 14. Summary of Chapter Seven

- Ezekiel describes a literal Millennial Temple in great detail.
- The Davidic Prince has unique responsibilities within this Temple.
- He leads worship, provides offerings, and represents the people.
- He alone sits in the Eastern Gate before Yahuah.
- He supports the sons of Zadok, who administer the holy things.
- The Temple becomes the spiritual and political heart of Yashar'el.
- Tribal allotments center around the sanctuary.
- The Dead Sea Scrolls parallel Ezekiel's vision closely.
- The Prince becomes the first non-priest restored to sacred proximity.
- The Temple merges heaven and earth, showcasing Yahuah's glory.

The Millennial Temple is the throne-room of Yahuah on earth, and the Prince is His chosen earthly administrator—fulfilling the ancient promises to David and restoring the worship system of Yashar'el in purity and holiness.

# CHAPTER EIGHT

# THE PRINCE AND THE TWELVE TRIBES: RESTORING THE NATION OF YASHAR'EL IN ITS ORIGINAL ORDER

One of the most powerful and foundational aspects of the latter-day restoration is the reunification and reordering of the **twelve tribes of Yashar'el.** The prophets speak with one voice: the end-time restoration is not merely spiritual—it is national, tribal, territorial, covenantal, and genealogical. The Prince, as the earthly ruler in the Kingdom Age, plays a central role in reassembling the scattered tribes and establishing them in their proper inheritance.

In this chapter we explore:
- The prophetic promise of tribal restoration
- The meaning of the two sticks (Ezekiel 37)
- The reunification of Judah and Ephraim
- The tribal allotment map in Ezekiel 48
- How the Prince administrates the restored tribal system
- The role of the priests, Levites, and sanctified districts
- Why territorial inheritance matters in the Kingdom
- Identity, genealogy, and diaspora return
- Tribal functions in the Millennial Kingdom
- The Dead Sea Scrolls' tribal expectations
- The Prince's authority over tribal chiefs
- How the restored tribes fulfill ancient covenant promises

This chapter shows how the Prince stands as the restorer of the national identity of Yashar'el, fulfilling the prophetic vision of unity and inheritance written thousands of years earlier.

## 1. The Promise of Tribal Restoration: A National Resurrection

The restoration of the twelve tribes is not metaphorical—it is physical and literal.

**Ezekiel 37:21–22 (KJV)**

*21 Behold, I will take the children of Israel from among the nations… and gather them on every side, and bring them into their own land.*

*22 And I will make them one nation… and one king shall be king to them all.*

Key facts:
- The gathering is **worldwide**
- The people return **to their land**
- The tribes become **one nation**
- A **Davidic king** rules them

This prophecy cannot be fulfilled without:
- Tribal identity
- Tribal unity

- Tribal inheritance
- A national leader

The Prince is that leader.

## 2. The Two Sticks Prophecy: Judah + Ephraim United

Perhaps the clearest description of restoration is the "Two Sticks" prophecy:

**Ezekiel 37:16–17**

*Take thee one stick, and write upon it, For Judah...*
*Then take another stick, For Joseph, the stick of Ephraim...*
*Join them one to another into one stick...*

**The two sticks represent:**
- Judah (Judah + Benjamin + Levi in exile)
- Ephraim (Northern tribes scattered by Assyria)

The reunification is supernatural:
- Yahuah Himself joins them
- No human effort can accomplish it
- It happens in the latter days

This reunification creates the national body the Prince will govern.

## 3. The Meaning of Tribal Restoration

Tribal restoration includes:

**A. Reclaiming heritage**

The tribes restore their ancient covenant identity.

**B. Returning to the land**

Geography is part of the covenant (Deut. 30:1–5).

**C. Receiving inheritance**

Each tribe receives its portion of land (Ezek. 48).

**D. Rebuilding national unity**

The Prince shepherds the people into oneness.

**E. Restoring the house of David**

The throne is only meaningful with a nation to govern.

**F. Reestablishing the priestly system**

Levites and Zadokites are restored in their roles.

Thus, tribal restoration is the backbone of the kingdom.

## 4. The Restoration Map: Ezekiel 48
Ezekiel provides a precise map of tribal allotments.
The order from north to south is:

1. Dan
2. Asher
3. Naphtali
4. Manasseh
5. Ephraim
6. Reuben
7. Judah

Then comes the holy district containing the:

- Sanctuary
- Priests' land
- Levites' land
- Temple complex
- Prince's land on both sides

South of that:

8. Benjamin
9. Simeon
10. Issachar
11. Zebulun
12. Gad

This layout is:

- Perfectly horizontal
- Egalitarian
- Territorial
- Divinely assigned

**No tribe is marginalized.**
**No tribe is lost.**
**No tribe is erased.**
The Prince's first task is overseeing this reallocation.


## 5. Why Does Tribal Land Matter in the Kingdom?
Some might ask:
**Why restore land? Why tribal boundaries? Why territorial inheritances?**

Because the covenant demands it.
### 1. Abrahamic Covenant
Land is part of the promise (Gen. 15:18).

**2. Mosaic Covenant**
Tribes inherit land by divine decree (Num. 34–36).
**3. Davidic Covenant**
A king needs a nation of tribes to rule.
**4. Prophets**
Isaiah, Jeremiah, Ezekiel, and Zechariah all emphasize land restoration.
**5. Yahuah's reputation**
Ezekiel 36 says the nations mock Yahuah when Israel is scattered.
Thus, land restoration vindicates His Name.
**6. Restoration of identity**
Israel's identity was tribal, not generic.
**7. Fulfillment of inheritance laws**
Every Israelite must have an inheritance in the land forever.
**8. The Prince preserves inheritance integrity**
He prevents land theft and corruption (Ezek. 46:18).
The Millennial Kingdom is rooted in land-based holiness.

## 6. The Prince's Administration of Tribal Restoration
The Prince plays a key role in many aspects of tribal life.
**A. Overseer of the tribal chiefs**
1QM 17 (War Scroll) says he is set "over all the leaders of the tribes."
**B. Guardian of inheritance**
He ensures the tribes receive their proper land.
**C. Preventer of oppression**
Ezekiel 45:9 commands him to prevent fraud and extortion.
**D. Protector of the people's land**
He may not seize land like past kings (Ezek. 46:18).
**E. Mediator between tribes and priests**
He administrates the civil matters; Zadok the spiritual.
**F. Organizer of worship gatherings**
He leads tribal delegations in feasts (Ezek. 46:10–11).
**G. Ensurer of balanced governance**
He enforces equal rights among tribes.
His leadership includes:
- Fairness
- Strength
- Wisdom
- Balance
- Loyalty to Torah

He is the anchor of national unity.

## 7. Restoring Priestly and Levitical Order

The Levites receive land within the holy district.
The sons of Zadok receive the inner sanctified territory.
This structure:

- Honors ancient Levitical calling
- Restores Torah-based hierarchy
- Separates the holy from the common
- Allows Yahuah's glory to remain

The Prince upholds this structure meticulously.
**He is the guardian of civil holiness; Zadok is the guardian of spiritual holiness.**

## 8. The Identity and Genealogy of the Tribes in the End-Time

Tribal identity is preserved through:

### A. Bloodline
The covenant specifies "zera"—physical descendants.

### B. Prophetic preservation
Yahuah promises He will not forget any tribe (Amos 9:9).

### C. Diaspora communities
Many tribes remained intact across Africa, Arabia, the Middle East, and the Diaspora.

### D. Divine regathering
No genealogical records are needed—Yahuah knows His people (Ezek. 37:12–14).

### E. The awakening
The Spirit reveals identity, as seen in modern movements returning to Israelite heritage.

### F. National repentance
Identity is restored through turning back to the covenant.
The Prince oversees the physical manifestation of this spiritual awakening.

## 9. Tribal Functions in the Millennial Kingdom

The tribes are not merely geographical—their functions remain.

### A. Judah
Leads praise, administration, and governance.

### B. Levi
Sanctifies worship and teaches Torah.

### C. Benjamin
Guards the sanctuary.

**D. Ephraim & Manasseh**
Agricultural and military strength.
**E. Zebulun**
Commerce and international trade.
**F. Issachar**
Wisdom, study, and times/seasons.
**G. Asher**
Oil and provision.
**H. Naphtali**
Freedom, eloquence, and swiftness.
**I. Gad**
Warriors and protectors of the border.
**J. Reuben**
Honor and firstborn rights (though transferred).
**K. Simeon**
Torah restoration and order.
Each tribe contributes uniquely to the kingdom's prosperity.

## 10. The Dead Sea Scrolls and Tribal Organization
The DSS reveal:
- The Qumran community anticipated a future tribal reorganization
- Priestly courses reflect expected national structure
- The War Scroll divides military units by tribes
- The Prince is set over the tribes
- The "twelve chiefs" of the tribes appear in Scroll texts
- The Davidic Messiah leads them in unity

This proves ancient Israelites expected the tribal system to be restored in the last days.

The Prince plays the same role Ezekiel describes—**Chief Overseer of the Tribes.**

## 11. The Prince and Tribal Unity
The Prince must:
**A. Heal ancient rivalries**
Judah vs. Ephraim was a historic division.
**B. Enforce fair boundaries**
No tribe may dominate another.
**C. Promote brotherhood**
The two sticks become one (Ezek. 37:17).

**D. Establish equal inheritance**

Each tribe receives equal horizontal strips of land.

**E. Ensure covenant fidelity**

He leads all twelve tribes in obedience to Torah.

**F. Restore justice between tribes**

He judges disputes in righteousness.

**G. Provide spiritual leadership**

Though not a priest, his leadership fosters covenant unity.

He becomes the **shepherd of all tribes simultaneously.**


## 12. The Restoration of the Tribes as the Fulfillment of Ancient Promise

From Genesis to Revelation, tribal restoration is a major theme.

**Abrahamic Covenant**

Land and descendants multiplied.

**Mosaic Covenant**

Inheritance laws for each tribe.

**Davidic Covenant**

A king ruling over a nation of tribes.

**Prophetic Writings**

Reunification of Judah and Ephraim.

**Ezekiel's Vision**

Tribal allotments surrounding the Temple.

**DSS Restoration Texts**

Twelve-tribe unity under a Davidic leader.

**Revelation 7**

The twelve tribes sealed at the end of days.

The Prince stands at the center of this fulfillment.


## 13. Summary of Chapter Eight

- The Prince's role is inseparable from the restoration of the twelve tribes.
- The two sticks prophecy (Ezek. 37) represents Judah and Ephraim's reunification.
- Ezekiel 48 outlines the exact territorial boundaries of each tribe.
- The Prince oversees tribal inheritance, unity, and governance.
- The priesthood is restored alongside the tribal structure.
- The tribes function in the Millennial Kingdom as they did in ancient
- days.
- The Dead Sea Scrolls confirm expectation of tribal restoration under
- a Davidic ruler.

- The Prince brings unity, justice, order, and covenant faithfulness.
- Tribal restoration fulfills the Abrahamic, Mosaic, and Davidic covenants.
- The end-time restoration is national, genealogical, territorial, and spiritual.

Restoring the tribes of Yashar'el is the climax of prophetic history—and the Davidic Prince is the shepherd and administrator of that restoration.

# CHAPTER NINE

# THE PRINCE AND THE NATIONS: HIS ROLE IN GLOBAL JUSTICE, PEACE, AND THE SUBMISSION OF THE GENTILES IN THE KINGDOM AGE

The rise of the Davidic Prince marks not only the restoration of Yashar'el but also a dramatic reordering of global power. The prophets consistently teach that the Kingdom of Yahuah—established in Jerusalem during the Millennial Reign—will transform the entire world. Nations will be judged, humbled, instructed, and brought into subjection to the rule of Yahuah through His divine Messiah and His appointed Davidic Prince.

In this chapter we explore:
- The prophetic role of the nations in the end-time scenario
- How the Davidic Prince relates to Gentile nations
- The global shift from worldly empires to Yahuah's kingdom
- The judgment of the nations
- The submission of the Gentiles to Yahuah
- The Prince's role in enforcing justice upon the nations
- The nations' pilgrimage to the House of Yahuah
- Torah going forth from Zion
- The global restoration of peace
- The role of the nations in the Millennial Kingdom
- How the Dead Sea Scrolls describe the nations in the final age
- The Prince's international authority under the divine King
- The final ingathering of the remnant from all nations

This chapter reveals how the Prince becomes an instrument of global justice, peace, and righteous administration under Messiah's eternal rule.

## 1. The Prophetic Role of the Nations in the Last Days

Scripture presents two categories of nations in the end times:

**A. Nations coming against Yashar'el**
- Gog's coalition in Ezekiel 38–39
- Nations gathered for judgment in Joel 3
- Nations provoking Jacob's Trouble
- Gentile powers that dominate until the Kingdom Age

**B. Nations submitting to Yahuah after judgment**
- Zechariah 14:16—Nations come yearly to worship
- Isaiah 2:2–4—Nations stream to Zion
- Isaiah 11:10—Gentiles seek the Root of Jesse
- Micah 4:1–5—Nations learn Torah from Zion

The Prince's role is deeply tied to the transition from category A to category B—helping the nations shift from rebellion to submission.

## 2. The Prince's Position in Global Governance

The divine Messiah reigns as the eternal sovereign.

Under Him, the Davidic Prince functions as:

- Vice-regent
- Governor of the Land of Israel
- Administrator of justice among the tribes
- Representative of Israel to the nations
- Enforcer of righteousness and peace

**The international order is centered on Zion.**

Isaiah 11, Ezekiel 37, and Zechariah 14 show that all nations:

- Recognize Yahuah
- Respect Israel
- Submit to His laws
- Seek instruction from Zion

The Prince helps administer this new world order.

## 3. The Collapse of Gentile Empires and Rise of Yahuah's Kingdom

Daniel interprets Nebuchadnezzar's dream of the statue (Dan. 2):

- Head of gold — Babylon
- Chest of silver — Medo-Persia
- Bronze belly — Greece
- Iron legs — Rome
- Iron & clay feet — divided kingdoms of the last days

Then comes a **stone cut without hands:**

### Daniel 2:44 (KJV)

*The Elohim of heaven shall set up a kingdom, which shall never be destroyed… it shall break in pieces and consume all these kingdoms, and it shall stand for ever.*

This stone symbolizes:

- The divine Messiah
- The establishment of Yahuah's eternal kingdom
- The restoration of the Davidic throne
- The end of Gentile rulership

The Prince functions within this indestructible Kingdom.

## 4. Judgment of the Nations

Many passages describe judgment before the Kingdom is fully established.

**Joel 3:1–2**

Nations judged for scattering Israel.

**Zephaniah 3:8**
Yahuah gathers nations for judgment.
**Isaiah 34**
Judgment on the nations who oppose Israel.
**Ezekiel 38–39**
Gog's coalition destroyed on the mountains of Israel.
**Zechariah 14:12–15**
Plague upon nations who attack Jerusalem.

This cleansing makes way for restored global order.
The Prince governs during the aftermath of this judgment, helping rebuild the world under Yahuah's laws.

**5. The Submission of the Nations**
After judgment, the redeemed nations voluntarily submit.
**Isaiah 2:2–3**
*Nations shall flow unto it… for out of Zion shall go forth the Torah.*
**Zechariah 8:23**
*Ten men from every nation shall take hold of the skirt of him that is a Jew (Israelite), saying, We will go with you.*
**Isaiah 11:10**
*To the Root of Jesse shall the Gentiles seek.*
**Micah 4:2**
Nations say, Teach us His ways.

The Prince plays a role in:
- Coordinating the nations' pilgrimages
- Ensuring peaceful international interactions
- Representing the throne of David to foreign peoples
- Preserving order during the transition

He is not king over the nations, but he is ruler **in the land** to which the nations come.

**6. The Prince's Role in International Justice**
Ezekiel shows him administering **internal justice** in Israel, but Isaiah and Micah imply Israel's rulers influence the nations.
The Prince's role includes:
**1. Upholding Torah justice in the land**
Foreigners living among Israel must follow the laws of Yahuah.

## 2. Protecting peaceful nations
Isaiah describes a world where nations no longer war.
## 3. Providing leadership for international worship
Nations join Israel during feasts.
## 4. Mediating disputes
The restored monarchy offers guidance to the world.
## 5. Enforcing sanctions
Zechariah 14:17—Nations refusing to worship lose rain.
The Prince participates in maintaining this order.

## 7. The Nations' Pilgrimage to Jerusalem
After the cleansing of the nations:
**All nations come to Jerusalem.**

### Zechariah 14:16
*Every one that is left of all the nations… shall go up from year to year to worship the King… and to keep the Feast of Tabernacles.*

### The Prince's responsibilities include:
- Overseeing logistics of the feast
- Partnering with priests for Temple worship
- Organizing tribal participation
- Ensuring order and peace
- Managing international entry protocols
- Representing Israel's civil government

This annual pilgrimage becomes the centerpiece of international unity.

## 8. Torah Goes Forth From Zion
During the Millennial Kingdom, the entire world is governed by the laws of Yahuah.
### Isaiah 2:3
*For out of Zion shall go forth the Torah, and the word of Yahuah from Jerusalem.*
### The Prince ensures:
- Proper teaching
- Proper administration
- Proper enforcement
- Proper worship
- Proper justice

This transforms nations from rebellion to righteousness.

## 9. Peace on Earth Under Yahuah's Government

Isaiah describes the world after divine intervention:

**Isaiah 2:4**

*They shall beat their swords into plowshares… nation shall not lift up sword against nation…*

**Peace emerges because:**

1. Nations worship Yahuah
2. The Prince administers justice
3. Torah governs the world
4. Messiah rules from Jerusalem
5. Violence is punished swiftly
6. Satan's influence is restrained
7. The people learn righteousness

The Prince oversees internal peace within Israel, which becomes a model for the nations.

## 10. The Role of Gentiles in the Millennial Kingdom

The prophets list several roles for Gentiles:

**A. Pilgrims and worshipers**

Zechariah 14:16—They keep Sukkot.

**B. Learners of Torah**

Isaiah 2:3—Teach us His ways.

**C. Builders and laborers**

Isaiah 60:10—Foreigners build your walls.

**D. Stewards and servants**

Isaiah 14:1–2—Nations serve Yashar'el.

**E. Supporters of Zion**

Isaiah 60:12—Nations who refuse perish.

**F. Participants in covenant peace**

They live under Yahuah's laws.

**G. Honorers of Israel's King**

Isaiah 60:14—They bow at Zion's feet.

The Prince governs their participation from the Israelite homeland.

## 11. The Dead Sea Scrolls' View of the Nations

The DSS anticipated:

- A final war between Israel and the Gentiles
- A Davidic Prince leading Israel to victory
- A priestly Messiah restoring holiness

- A future age of peace after war
- Gentile nations acknowledging Yahuah
- The submission of foreign kings
- The elevation of Israel as head and not tail

**1QM (War Scroll) describes:**
- Nations defeated by Yahuah
- Peace under the Prince's rule
- An era of righteousness

This reinforces the prophetic worldview found in Ezekiel, Isaiah, and Micah.

## 12. The Prince's International Authority Under Messiah

The Prince is not the universal king—that role belongs to the divine Messiah.

But the Prince is:
- King over Israel
- Administrator of justice in Zion
- Gatekeeper for international worship
- Leader of the unified tribes
- Overseer of national and international feasts
- Representative of Israel to all nations
- Chief diplomat of Zion
- Enforcer of covenant law within the land

He is the world's most influential mortal ruler.

## 13. The Final Ingathering of the Remnant

The restoration of the tribes comes from **all nations.**

**Isaiah 11:11–12**

Yahuah gathers Israel from:
- The islands
- The coasts
- The nations
- The four corners of the earth

The Prince oversees:
- Their resettlement
- Their inheritance
- Their integration
- Their restoration to tribal order

This is the last stage of global redemption.

## 14. Summary of Chapter Nine

- The nations are judged in the end times for their treatment of Israel.
- After judgment, the redeemed nations submit to Yahuah.
- The Prince governs Israel as nations stream to Zion for worship.
- Torah goes forth into all the earth from Jerusalem.
- The Prince administers justice and peace under the divine King.
- The nations keep the Feast of Tabernacles annually.
- Gentile nations accept Israel's leadership in the Kingdom Age.
- The Dead Sea Scrolls affirm a Davidic Prince overseeing this
- transformation.
- The Prince becomes international diplomat, judge, and shepherd of
- the restored nation.
- The world experiences true peace and righteousness for the first
- time.

The Davidic Prince stands at the center of global restoration, guiding both Israel and the nations into the era of peace, holiness, and truth under Yahuah's eternal Kingdom.

# CHAPTER TEN

# THE IDENTITY, SIGNS, AND RECOGNITION OF THE END-TIME DAVIDIC PRINCE: A PROPHETIC PORTRAIT FOR THE LAST GENERATION

The prophetic warnings, promises, and revelations regarding the end-time Davidic Prince reach their climax in the question that has stirred believers for centuries: **How will Yashar'el recognize this ruler when he arrives?** Scripture speaks of his character, his mission, his heart, his authority, his connection to the Messiah, and his role in the Millennial Kingdom—but it also gives clues regarding the **timing, circumstances,** and **signs** surrounding his rise.

This chapter explores:
- The mystery of the Prince's identity
- Why Yahuah conceals him until the appointed time
- The prophetic and historical patterns of hidden leaders
- The personal qualities that distinguish the Prince
- The signs given in Scripture
- The role of suffering and refining
- The calling and anointing of the Prince
- His relationship with the remnant
- The recognition of the Prince by Yashar'el
- False princes and deceivers in the last days
- How the Dead Sea Scrolls describe the Prince's emergence
- The Prince's rise during global shaking
- What the awakened remnant should be watching for
- The ultimate purpose of the Prince in Yahuah's plan

This chapter brings together all threads of prophecy into a final, vivid portrait of the Prince's identity and mission.

## 1. The Mystery of the Prince's Identity
Unlike the divine Messiah—whose identity, titles, and mission are woven clearly throughout Scripture—the Prince's identity is **deliberately concealed.**
**Why?**
Because his calling is:
- Human
- Earthly
- Tribal
- Generational
- Connected to diaspora trauma
- In need of divine protection
- Hidden until the nation is ready

Yahuah hides His servants until the appointed time:
- Moses hidden 80 years
- David hidden in the fields
- Joseph hidden in prison
- Gideon hidden in the winepress
- Jephthah hidden in exile
- Jeremiah hidden from persecution
- Ezra and Nehemiah hidden in captivity

The Prince follows this pattern.

## 2. Why Yahuah Conceals Him Until the Appointed Time
Prophecy stresses that the Prince is:
- "Raised up" (Jer. 30:9)
- "Set over" the flock (Ezek. 34:23)
- "Established" as Prince (Ezek. 37:24)
- "Appointed" in the Covenant of Peace (Ezek. 37:26)

His rise is an **act of divine timing,** not human recognition.

**Reasons for concealment:**
**A. Protection from persecution**
Satan always attacks the seed before the mission matures.
**B. Protection from pride**
Yahuah elevates humble men.
**C. Preparation through suffering**
Leaders are forged in adversity.
**D. The nation must awaken before it can recognize him**
Hosea 3:5—Israel seeks Yahuah after awakening.
**E. The Prince rises after Jacob's Trouble**
Jer. 30:7–9 shows the Prince appears after deep suffering.

Yahuah unveils him only when:
- The remnant is awakened
- The tribes are gathering
- The nation is humbled
- The people are ready for righteous leadership

## 3. Prophetic Patterns of Hidden Leaders
Every great Israelite leader was:
- Humble
- Unknown

- Unexpected
- Raised from lowliness
- Surprising to the nation
- Overlooked by the elite

**David**
Ignored even by his own father.
**Moses**
Exiled in Midian.
**Joseph**
Buried in prison.
**Gideon**
Threshing wheat in secret.
**Jephthah**
Driven away as an outcast.
**Samuel**
A miracle child from a barren woman.
**Joshua**
Raised quietly under Moses.
**Zerubbabel**
A humble governor restoring broken ruins.
These patterns reveal a consistent truth:
**Yahuah chooses men the world ignores.**
The Prince is no exception.


## 4. The Personal Qualities That Distinguish the Prince
Scripture presents his character repeatedly:
**A. Humility**
He serves rather than rules with arrogance.
**B. Righteousness**
He follows Torah and leads others into it.
**C. Courage**
He stands firm during crisis and tribulation.
**D. Compassion**
He is a shepherd, not a tyrant.
**E. Justice**
He hates oppression (Ezek. 45:9).
**F. Integrity**
He refuses corruption and bribery.
**G. Wisdom**
He judges disputes in truth and fairness.

**H. Zeal for Yahuah**
He loves holiness and hates idolatry.
**I. Faithfulness**
He walks in obedience consistently.
**J. Sacrifice**
He is willing to give his life for the nation.
These qualities make him recognizable to the righteous remnant.


## 5. Signs Given in Scripture for Identifying the Prince
Though his identity is hidden, Scripture gives clues:
**1. Lineage of David**
He descends from the royal house.
**2. Appears in the last days**
After the awakening and regathering (Hosea 3:5).
**3. Raised up by Yahuah**
Not chosen by elections or political movements.
**4. Appears among the remnant**
Ezek. 34:23—He is "one of them."
**5. Leads a repentant people**
Hosea 3:5—Israel returns in fear and trembling.
**6. Connected to the Covenant of Peace**
Ezek. 37:26—His installation is tied to the covenant.
**7. Coexists with the rebuilt Temple**
Ezek. 45–46.
**8. Identified with "David My Servant"**
A title always referring to a mortal, anointed ruler.
**9. A shepherd's heart**
Ezek. 34:23—He feeds the flock.
**10. Recognized through spirit, not spectacle**
He is revealed by obedience, not by charisma.
These signs form the prophetic criteria for recognition.


## 6. The Role of Suffering and Refining in the Prince's Preparation
The Prince, like David, is shaped through:
- Hardship
- Rejection
- False accusations
- Poverty or displacement
- Loneliness
- Battle

- Spiritual encounters
- Unexpected deliverances

This refining is necessary because:
- Trials produce humility
- Suffering produces compassion
- Struggle produces endurance
- Scorn produces wisdom
- Tribulation produces purity
- Testing produces discernment

The Prince emerges from fire refined like gold.

## 7. The Calling and Anointing of the Prince
The Prince's anointing is:
**A. Sovereign**
Yahuah chooses him.
**B. Spiritual**
The Spirit comes upon him like David (1 Sam. 16:13).
**C. Covenant-based**
Rooted in promises to David's house.
**D. Recognized by the righteous**
The remnant perceives his call.
**E. Confirmed by obedience**
His character proves his anointing.
**F. Empowered by divine protection**
Enemies cannot remove him.
**G. Gradual but undeniable**
He rises like dawn—slow at first, then bright.
Anointing makes the Prince capable of stewarding Yahuah's Kingdom.

## 8. His Relationship with the Remnant
The Prince is connected to:
**A. The broken**
He binds the wounded (Ezek. 34:16).
**B. The scattered**
He gathers them home.
**C. The faithful**
He leads them into deeper obedience.
**D. The awakened**
He strengthens their identity.

**E. The righteous**

They recognize his calling.

**F. The covenant-keepers**

They stand with him.

He does not rule over strangers—he shepherds the awakened House of Yashar'el.

## 9. How Yashar'el Recognizes the Prince

The remnant recognizes him not through:

- Flattery
- Crowds
- Media
- Political power
- Outward glory

The recognition is spiritual:

**1. Through signs**

His life aligns with prophecy.

**2. Through fruit**

His righteousness is evident.

**3. Through suffering**

He has endured without losing faith.

**4. Through humility**

He magnifies Yahuah, not himself.

**5. Through Spirit**

The Ruach HaQodesh testifies in the remnant.

**6. Through obedience**

He walks in Torah faithfully.

**7. Through character**

His heart matches David's.

This recognition is essential for national unity.

## 10. False Princes and Deceivers in the Last Days

Scripture warns of:

- False shepherds
- Corrupt leaders
- Oppressors
- Deceivers
- False messiahs
- Political pretenders
- Charismatic impostors

The true Prince stands out because:
- He never oppresses
- He never manipulates
- He never exalts himself
- He never violates Torah
- He never deviates from righteousness
- He never harms the flock

He shepherds, not devours.

## 11. How the Dead Sea Scrolls Describe the Prince's Emergence

In the DSS, the Prince is:
- Appointed by Yahuah (1QM 17)
- Set over tribal leaders
- A warrior of righteousness
- Humble
- A leader during eschatological conflict
- Working with a priestly Messiah
- Recognized by the community of the faithful
- Opposed by wicked nations
- Vindicated by divine intervention

His emergence echoes David's rise: sudden, surprising, unstoppable.

## 12. The Prince's Rise During Global Shaking

Scripture places his rise during:
- War
- Chaos
- Distress
- Natural upheavals
- Judgment
- Global conflict
- Identity awakening
- Political collapse
- Religious deception
- Persecution
- National repentance

The Prince steps forward when the world collapses, not when it prospers.

### 13. What the Remnant Should Watch For
**A. Global awakening of Israelite identity**
Hosea 3:5.
**B. Return to Torah**
Jer. 31:31–34; Ezek. 36:27.
**C. Reuniting of Judah and Ephraim**
Ezek. 37:15–22.
**D. National repentance**
Hosea 5:15.
**E. Jacob's Trouble**
Jer. 30:7.
**F. Divine deliverance**
Jer. 30:10.
**G. Restoration of the land**
Ezek. 36.
**H. Rebuilding of the Temple**
Ezek. 40–48.
**I. Appointment of the Prince**
Ezek. 34:23; 37:24.
When these converge, the Prince is revealed.

### 14. The Ultimate Purpose of the Prince in Yahuah's Plan
He exists to:
- Shepherd Yashar'el
- Unite the tribes
- Restore justice
- Prepare the nation for divine presence
- Maintain the covenant
- Govern righteously
- Represent the people
- Uphold holiness
- Administer Temple worship
- Establish peace
- Guide the nations in righteousness

He is the final earthly king of Yashar'el before eternity merges with time.
He is:
- A servant
- A shepherd
- A warrior
- A father to the nation

- A son of David
- A man after Yahuah's own heart
- A prince forever (Ezek. 37:25)

## 15. Summary of Chapter Ten
- Scripture conceals the Prince's identity until the last days.
- He is revealed through righteousness, humility, and divine timing.
- He rises during global distress and Israel's national awakening.
- His character mirrors David's heart.
- He shepherds the remnant and leads tribal restoration.
- He upholds Torah and partners with the priesthood.
- The nations recognize Yahuah's kingdom through his leadership.
- The Dead Sea Scrolls support a hidden, rising Prince in the end time.
- The Prince's purpose is to restore order, justice, worship, and unity.
- He is the final earthly ruler of Yashar'el under the eternal King.

This prophetic portrait forms the climax of the entire book.

CONCLUSION

# THE RETURN OF THE KINGDOM AND THE RISE OF THE PRINCE: THE RESTORATION OF YASHAR'EL IN THE AGE OF REDEMPTION

The journey through the prophetic scriptures—from the writings of Hosea, Jeremiah, Isaiah, Ezekiel, Zechariah, to the imagery preserved in the Dead Sea Scrolls—reveals a breathtaking, unified vision: **the complete restoration of the Kingdom of Yashar'el under the governance of Yahuah, the reign of His divine Messiah, and the stewardship of His earthly Davidic Prince.**

This conclusion brings together the threads of all previous chapters, showing how every prophecy, covenant, and historical pattern converges into a single, magnificent purpose: **the rebirth of a holy nation that reflects the glory of Yahuah to all the earth.**

## 1. The Restoration Story Is the Story of Yashar'el

From the moment Yashar'el was scattered among the nations, the prophets saw a future where the people would:

- Awaken
- Remember
- Repent
- Seek Yahuah
- Return to covenant
- Reclaim identity
- Rebuild unity
- Regather from the four corners of the earth
- Reestablish tribal order
- Receive righteous leadership
- Become a kingdom of priests and a set-apart nation

This is not metaphorical. It is literal.

- It is national.
- It is historical.
- It is genealogical.
- It is spiritual.
- It is territorial.
- It is covenantal.
- It is the destiny of the twelve tribes of Yashar'el.

And at the center of this restoration stands **the Prince,** Yahuah's chosen servant and shepherd.

## 2. The Davidic Prince: The Covenant Shepherd of the Last Days

The Prince is not Messiah, yet he is indispensable to the Kingdom. He is not divine, yet he is filled with the Spirit. He is not the High Priest, yet he approaches the presence in the Eastern Gate. He is not the eternal King, yet he is king over the united tribes.

He is:

- "My servant David"
- "One shepherd over them all"
- "Their leader forever"
- "My Prince"
- "The overseer over My people"

His role is both humble and exalted, both pastoral and royal, both administrative and spiritual.

He restores:

- Unity
- Justice
- Tribal inheritance
- Temple order
- Covenant faithfulness
- National righteousness

He is the embodiment of what a righteous leader should be.

## 3. The Covenant of Peace: The Foundation of the New Kingdom

One of the most profound revelations in Ezekiel is the **Covenant of Peace.**
This covenant is:

- Everlasting
- Restorative
- Just
- Holy
- Centered on the sanctuary
- Governed by the Prince
- Administered by the Zadokite priesthood
- Anchored in the presence of Yahuah

Through this covenant:

- The land is healed
- The people are unified
- The sanctuary is restored
- Oppression is ended
- Justice flows like water
- Yahuah dwells among His people forever

The Prince is the earthly executor of this covenant.

## 4. The Temple: The Heart of the Kingdom

The Millennial Temple described by Ezekiel is the apex of divine-human interaction. It is where:

- Heaven and earth intersect
- Yahuah's glory returns
- Worship is purified
- The nations come to learn Torah
- The Prince sits in the Eastern Gate
- The priests minister in holiness
- The people gather in unity
- The world witnesses the presence of Yahuah

The Temple is not merely a building.
It is the throne-room of the Kingdom of Yahuah.

## 5. The Reunification of the Twelve Tribes

The two sticks—Judah and Ephraim—becoming one is the heartbeat of the entire prophetic restoration.
This reunification means:

- An end to ancient hostility
- Restoration of tribal identity
- Reinstitution of inheritance
- Rebuilding of national unity
- Healing of historical wounds
- Reconstruction of the House of David
- Bringing together of all Yah-fearing Israelites scattered across the earth

The Prince is the shepherd who guides this restored nation into its destiny.

## 6. The Nations Brought Under the Rule of Yahuah

The prophets declare that the nations will experience:

- Judgment
- Refining
- Submission
- Worship
- Instruction
- Peace
- Accountability under Torah
- Participation in the Feast of Tabernacles
- Respect for Zion

137

The world's political systems will collapse, but the Kingdom of Yahuah will stand forever.

Gentile nations shall say:
**"Come, let us go up to the mountain of Yahuah... for out of Zion shall go forth the Torah."**
The Prince is the administrator of righteousness in the land from which the nations learn.

### 7. The Purpose of the Prince in Yahuah's Eternal Plan
The Prince is central to the age of redemption because:
**A. He embodies the heart of David**
A shepherd-king, humble and faithful.
**B. He unites the tribes**
Healing ancient divisions.
**C. He enforces justice**
Stopping oppression and injustice.
**D. He protects inheritance rights**
Ensuring every family in Yashar'el receives its portion.
**E. He leads national worship**
Representing the people before Yahuah.
**F. He stabilizes the land**
Bringing peace and security.
**G. He partners with the priesthood**
Maintaining purity in worship.
**H. He upholds Torah**
Ensuring covenant obedience.
**I. He oversees Temple worship**
Following Yahuah's ordinances precisely.
**J. He prepares Yashar'el for the presence of Yahuah**
Making the land ready for divine habitation.
The Prince is Yahuah's chosen vessel to complete the earthly restoration before eternity begins.

### 8. The Return of Divine Presence:
Yahuah Dwelling Among His People
All prophecy leads to this climax:
\*\***"My sanctuary shall be in the midst of them forevermore...**
and the nations shall know that I, Yahuah, sanctify Yashar'el."\*\*
(Ezek. 37:26–28)

The return of the divine presence:
- Sanctifies the land
- Confirms the covenant
- Validates the Prince's installation
- Reveals Yahuah's love
- Announces the victory of His Kingdom
- Begins the age of eternal peace

This is the fulfillment of every promise given to:
- Abraham
- Isaac
- Jacob
- The Prophets
- The Psalms
- David
- he faithful remnant

The Prince stands as the first restored ruler under this eternal presence.

## 9. The Destiny of Yashar'el: A Kingdom of Priests, A Light to the Nations

At last, the identity of Yashar'el is restored.

**Not a scattered people,**

**Not an oppressed remnant,**

**Not a forgotten nation,**

**But the Kingdom of Yahuah on earth.**

Under Messiah's eternal rule
and the Prince's earthly stewardship,

Yashar'el becomes:
- A light to the Gentiles
- A nation walking in righteousness
- A people restored to covenant
- A family reunited in tribal order
- A witness to Yahuah's holiness
- A beacon of justice
- A kingdom set apart
- A testimony to the nations

The age of redemption transforms the world through the restoration of Yashar'el.

## 10. The Final Word: Hope for the Last Generation

As we stand in the unfolding of prophetic times, several truths shine brightly:

**1. The awakening of Yashar'el has begun.**

Identity is returning to scattered descendants worldwide.

**2. The Spirit of Yahuah is stirring the remnant.**

A hunger for Torah, righteousness, and truth is rising.

**3. The nations are trembling.**

The world systems are collapsing as prophecy foretold.

**4. The stage for Jacob's Trouble is forming.**

Scripture's warnings echo in modern events.

**5. The restoration of the tribal order is approaching.**

Ezekiel's map awaits fulfillment.

**6. The Millennial Temple stands in vision, ready to be revealed.**

Yahuah's glory will return.

**7. The Davidic Prince will rise when the nation is ready.**

A man of humility, righteousness, and covenant fidelity.

**8. The return of the divine King is certain.**

Messiah will reign forever.

**9. Yahuah's promises cannot fail.**

He has spoken; He will perform it.

**10. The Kingdom is coming.**

And Yashar'el will be restored.

The Divine Plan is unfolding.
The Kingdom is imminent.
The Prince will rise.
The tribes will return.
The Temple will stand.
The nations will bow.
And Yahuah will dwell among His people forever.
This is the destiny of Yashar'el.
This is the hope of the remnant.
This is the promise of Yahuah.

# BIBLIOGRAPHY
*Primary Sources, Secondary Sources, and Supporting Literature*

## I. SCRIPTURE (PRIMARY SOURCES)
Hebrew Scriptures / Tanakh
- *Genesis* – Bereshith
- *Exodus* – Shemoth
- *Leviticus* – Vayiqra
- *Numbers* – Bemidbar
- *Deuteronomy* – Devarim
- *Joshua* – Yehoshua
- *Judges* – Shoftim
- *1–2 Samuel* – Shemu'el
- *1–2 Kings* – Melakhim
- *1–2 Chronicles* – Divrei Hayamim
- *Psalms* – Tehillim
- *Isaiah* – Yeshayahu
- *Jeremiah* – Yirmeyahu
- *Lamentations* – Eichah
- *Ezekiel* – Yechezqel
- *Daniel* – Daniyel
- *Hosea* – Hoshea
- *Joel* – Yo'el
- *Amos*
- *Micah* – Mikah
- *Zephaniah* – Tsephanyah
- *Zechariah* – Zekaryah
- *Malachi* – Mal'akhi

### Brit HaDashah (New Testament)
(for theological correlation only; not doctrinally required)
- *Matthew, Luke* – genealogies of David
- *Acts 15* – restoration of the tabernacle of David
- *Revelation 7 & 21* – twelve tribes, New Jerusalem

## II. APOCRYPHA (SECOND TEMPLE LITERATURE)
- *1 Esdras*

- *2 Esdras (4 Ezra)*
- *Tobit*
- *Judith*
- *Wisdom of Solomon*
- *Sirach (Ecclesiasticus)*
- *Baruch*
- *Letter of Jeremiah*
- *Prayer of Manasseh*
- *1–4 Maccabees*

## III. PSEUDEPIGRAPHA (INTERTESTAMENTAL WORKS)
### A. Messianic & Eschatological Texts
- *1 Enoch (Ethiopian Enoch)*
- *2 Enoch (Slavonic Enoch)*
- *3 Enoch (Hebrew Enoch)*
- *Book of Jubilees*
- *Testaments of the Twelve Patriarchs*
- *Psalms of Solomon (especially Psalm 17 & 18 on the Davidic*
- *Messiah)*
- *The Sibylline Oracles*
- *The Apocalypse of Abraham*
- *The Ladder of Jacob*
- *The Apocalypse of Zephaniah*
- *The Apocalypse of Baruch (2 Baruch)*
- *The Book of Adam and Eve*
- *The Martyrdom and Ascension of Isaiah*

### B. Davidic/Messianic Emphasis Texts
- *2 Baruch 70–72 – restoration of the Kingdom*
- *4 Ezra 11–13 – the man from the sea (messianic figure)*
- *Testament of Judah – warrior messiah imagery*
- *Testament of Levi – priestly messiah insights*
- *Pseudo-Philo*

## IV. DEAD SEA SCROLLS (QUMRAN TEXTS)
*(Primary sources regarding the Prince of the Congregation, Davidic ruler, and dual-Messiah expectation)*

### A. Messianic Prophecy & Davidic Prince Texts
- **1QM – The War Scroll**

*Rule of the War of the Sons of Light Against the Sons of Darkness*
*Key sections: 1QM 5, 7, 11, 17 – mentions the "Prince of the*
*Congregation."*

- **1QSa – Rule of the Congregation**

Describes the Messiah of Israel and the Messiah of Aaron.

- **1QS – Community Rule**

Mentions the Messiahs of Aaron and Israel (1QS IX, 11).

- **4Q174 – Florilegium (Midrash on the Last Days)**

Identifies the Branch of David from 2 Samuel 7.

- **4Q285 – The Pierced Messiah / Branch of David Fragment**

Links the Davidic ruler with eschatological warfare.

- **4Q161 – Isaiah Pesher**

Commentary identifying the Branch of David in Isaiah 11.

- **4Q252 – Commentary on Genesis**

Includes references to the future Davidic ruler.

- **11QTemple (Temple Scroll)**

Anticipates a future holy sanctuary and purified Temple.

- **4Q521 – The Messianic Apocalypse**

Anticipates miracles and restoration parallel to Davidic and priestly
messianic expectations.

## V. HISTORICAL & ANCIENT SOURCES

- **Josephus, Flavius**
  *Antiquities of the Jews*
  *The Jewish War*
- **Philo of Alexandria**
  *On Rewards and Punishments*
  *On the Embassy to Gaius*
- **Tacitus**
  *Histories* — *reference to first-century messianic expectations.*
- **The Targums**
  *Targum Jonathan on Isaiah (messianic interpretations)*
  *Targum Psalms*
- **The Mishnah & Talmud (select passages)**
  *Sanhedrin 98 – discussions of the Messiah*
  *Sukkah 52 – lamentation for "the pierced one"*

## VI. MODERN SCHOLARSHIP (BACKGROUND & CONTEXT)

*(Useful for understanding the prophetic, archaeological, and historical*
*framework of the Davidic Prince; all can be included in a bibliography*

*even if not directly quoted.)*

## A. Israelite & Ancient Near Eastern Background
- Albright, W.F. *Yahweh and the Gods of Canaan.*
- Bright, John. *A History of Israel.*
- Cross, Frank Moore. *Canaanite Myth and Hebrew Epic.*

## B. Dead Sea Scroll Studies
- Vermes, Geza. *The Complete Dead Sea Scrolls in English.*
- Wise, Abegg & Cook. *The Dead Sea Scrolls: A New Translation.*
- Schiffman, Lawrence. *Reclaiming the Dead Sea Scrolls.*
- García Martínez, Florentino. *The Dead Sea Scrolls Study Edition.*

## C. Davidic & Messianic Scholarship
- Kaiser, Walter C. *The Messiah in the Old Testament.*
- Collins, John J. *The Scepter and the Star.*
- Rydelnik, Michael. *The Messianic Hope.*

## D. Ezekiel & Prophetic Literature
- Block, Daniel I. *The Book of Ezekiel* (NICOT Commentary).
- Duguid, Iain. *Ezekiel.*
- Wright, Christopher. *The Message of Ezekiel.*

## E. Restorationism & End-Time Prophecy
- Motyer, J.A. *The Prophecy of Isaiah.*
- Waltke, Bruce K. *An Old Testament Theology.*

## VII. AFRICAN, DIASPORA, AND HEBREW ISRAELITE STUDIES
*(Historical context for scattered tribes and diaspora movements.)*
- Williams, Chancellor. The Destruction of Black Civilization.
- Snowden, Frank. Blacks in Antiquity.
- Goldenberg, David. The Curse of Ham: Race and Slavery in Early
- Judaism, Christianity, and Islam.
- ben-Jochannan, Yosef. Black Man of the Nile.
- Rudolph Windsor. From Babylon to Timbuktu.
- Parfitt, Tudor. Black Jews in Africa and the Americas.
- Falola, Toyin & Childs, Matt. West African Diaspora.

## VIII. CARTOGRAPHIC & HISTORICAL GEOGRAPHY SOURCES
(relevant for restoring tribal land maps and understanding Ezekiel 48)
- John Ogilby. Africa: Being an Accurate Description of the Regions.
- (17th century)
- Abraham Ortelius. Theatrum Orbis Terrarum.

- Blaeu, Joan. Atlas Maior.
- Britannica Atlases (historical editions)
- Ptolemy. Geographia.

## IX. OTHER WORKS OF RELEVANCE

- The Book of Jasher (Sefer HaYashar)
- The Book of Adam and Eve
- The Book of the Cave of Treasures
- The Book of the Bee
- The Damascus Document (CD)
- The Community Rule (1QS)
- The Rule of the Congregation (1QSa)
- The War Scroll (1QM)
- The Temple Scroll (11QT)

## X. DIGITAL AND RESEARCH RESOURCES

- Israel Antiquities Authority (IAA) — Dead Sea Scrolls Digital Library
- The Leon Levy DSS Project
- The Biblical Archaeology Society Library
- The Oriental Institute, University of Chicago
- The Center for Online Judaic Studies
- The Online Critical Pseudepigrapha Project